SECLUDED ISLANDS

of the

ATLANTIC COAST

SECLUDED ISLANDS
of the
ATLANTIC COAST

Written and illustrated by
David Yeadon

Crown Publishers, Inc., New York

By the same author

Hidden Corners of Britain (George Allen and Unwin; W.W. Norton 1981)

Hidden Corners of Southern Europe (Harper & Row 1981)

Backroad Journeys of the West Coast States (Harper & Row 1979)

When the Earth was Young (Doubleday 1979)

Nooks and Crannies of New York City (Charles Scribner 1979)

Hidden Corners of the MidAtlantic States (Funk and Wagnalls 1977)

Hidden Corners of New England (Funk and Wagnalls 1976)

New York Book of Bars, Pubs and Taverns (Hawthorn 1975)

Sumptuous Indulgence on a Shoestring (a cookbook) (Hawthorn 1974)

Wine Tasting in California (Camaro 1973)

Hidden Restaurants of California (2 vols) (Camaro 1972)

Exploring Small Towns of California (2 vols) (Ward Ritchie 1972)

Copyright © 1984 by David Yeadon
All rights reserved. No part of this book may be reproduced or transmitted in any form or by any means, electronic or mechanical, including photocopying, recording, or by any information storage and retrieval system, without permission in writing from the publisher.
Published by Crown Publishers, Inc.,
One Park Avenue, New York, New York 10016,
and simultaneously in Canada
by General Publishing Company Limited
Manufactured in the United States of America

Library of Congress Cataloging in Publication Data

Yeadon, David.
    Secluded Islands of the Atlantic Coast.

    1. Atlantic Coast (U.S.)—Description and travel—Guide-books.   2. Atlantic Coast (Canada)—Description and travel—Guide-books.   3. Islands—Atlantic Coast (U.S.)—Guide-books.   4. Islands—Atlantic Coast (Canada)—Guide-books.   I. Title.
F106.Y43   1984   917.1'044'09142   84-1793
ISBN 0-517-54365-6

10 9 8 7 6 5 4 3 2 1
First Edition

for my mother
*—world traveler
and friend*

WORDS OF THANKS

Scores of people showed kindness during my travels and many others contributed to the completion of the book. In particular I would like to thank:

Jim & Carol Alberto - for sharing their love of Daufuskie.
Eric Allaby - curator of the Grand Manan museum.
Bill & Natalie Bacon - for an afternoon of wine-tasting on Prudence.
Jim Bock - for sharing his hopes with me on Swan's Island.
Vernon Bradshaw - for island insights on Tangier.
John T. Capps III - founder of Bald Headed Men of America.
Ruth Danon - for careful and enthusiastic copy editing.
John Fowles - author, whose book on "Islands" gave me inspiration.
Gleason Green - for his tales of the lobstering life on Grand Manan.
Penny Haythorn - for the best guided tour of the journey, on Sapelo.
Lisa Healy - my new editor, for her patience and enthusiasm.
Ame Herrera - for her suggestions and improvements to the book.
Fritz Johnson - for his tales of the quarryman's life on Swan's Island.
Frances Kitching - for her hospitality on Smith Island.
Don Kosin - for his help in exploring Big Pine.
Frederic Landry - for his kindnesses on the Magdalens.
Edward Hammonds - for his suggestions and improvements to the book.
Paul McVane - for his hospitality on Cliff Island.
Carl Nelson - for his company on Great Cranberry.
Nu-Wave Graphics - for the hard work of Emil, Lori and Mike.
Peacock Publishing - for the always cheerful Angelo and Bernie.
Andre Racz - for showing me Vinalhaven's secret places.
Mack Riddel - for his help on Cape Lookout.
Tony Seamon - for his insights on Cape Lookout.
Guy Scarpino - for his life story on Vinalhaven.
Hilbert Schenck - for his word-pictures of Cuttyhunk life.
Bob Simpson - for his stories of Cape Lookout.
True Sims - for coordinating production so effectively.
Paul Stockbridge - for (almost) a day lobstering on Swan's Island.
The Stevens - for sharing their love of Cuttyhunk.
Bill Sweetland - for fresh cod and good conversation on Monhegan.

Rudy Thomas - for my initiation into the world of crabs, in Crisfield.
Alan Tyler - for a most entertaining ride to Smith Island.
Hugh Van Dusen - editor and friend, who gives good advice.
Johanna Von Tiling - for her company on Cliff Island.
Nach Waxman - my original editor on the project.
Larry Williams - for his hospitality on Ocracoke,

and of course, my wife, **Anne Yeadon**
         —for everything.

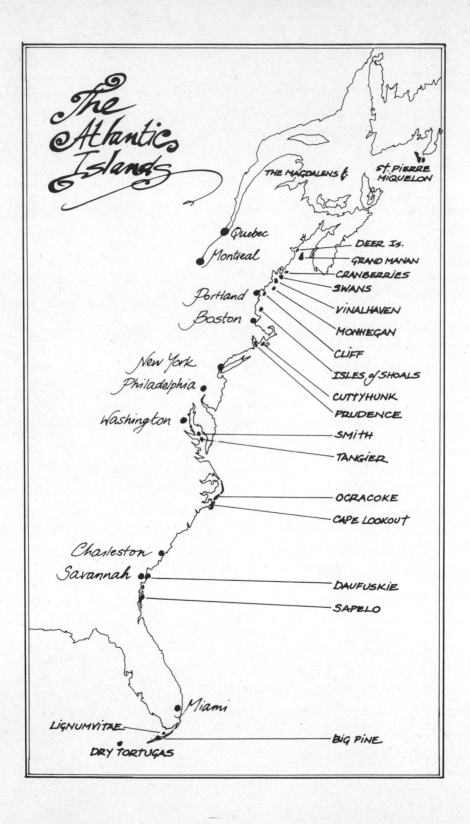

The Atlantic Islands

THE MAGDALENS &
St. PIERRE MIQUELON

Quebec
Montreal

DEER Is.
GRAND MANAN
CRANBERRIES
SWANS
Portland
Boston
VINALHAVEN
MONHEGAN
CLIFF
ISLES of SHOALS
New York
Philadelphia
CUTTYHUNK
PRUDENCE
Washington
SMITH
TANGIER

OCRACOKE
CAPE LOOKOUT

Charleston
Savannah
DAUFUSKIE
SAPELO

Miami
LIGNUMVITAE
BIG PINE
DRY TORTUGAS

Contents

An Invitation to Islands

"Away with a corrupt world!
Let us breathe the air of enchanted islands."

George Meredith, 1828—1909

And they are truly enchanted—these 3,000 or so fragments of ancient mountain tops, sandbars, and reefs that make up the Atlantic islands of America's east coast.

I chose a modest twenty-one to explore and enjoy. I looked for places with indigenous populations, working islands with traditions, legends and secrets, places slow to adopt the new ways of "comers-in." I looked for "character"—the subtle result of symbiosis between inhabitants, land, and ocean. I looked for contrast; my islands range from tiny rocky outcrops, treeless and lost in long winters, to the pine-profiled archipelago of Maine and soft Southern isles snoozing in the shade of live oaks and spanish moss. I traveled from those misty "fragments of France" off the Newfoundland coast, St. Pierre-Miquelon, all the way to the Dry Tortugas at the farthest tip of the Florida Keys.

It was a long journey broken by intervals in the New York metropolis. Sometimes I welcomed the breaks and enjoyed the city's hullaballo and its sophisticated comforts. Most times I missed the silences, and the simple life of my islands. I carried memories with me on the crowded avenues—memories of being lost on Miquelon's desolate "mornes," memories of the great sandy strands of the Magdalens, the aroma of herring smokehouses on Grand Manan, a day of lobstering on Swan's Island in Maine, the old granite quarrymen on Vinalhaven, the genteel residents of Monhegan, the winemakers of Prudence, the crabmen of Chesapeake Bay, the strange black Gullah-speaking citizens of Daufuskie, the 1,500 year old trees on Lignumvitae, and the great blue spaces of the Dry Tortugas. Hundreds of memories from hundreds of days out among the islands.

But islands are not for everyone. When the ferry leaves, many visitors feel abandoned, stranded in tatters of woods tied together by sandy tracks, floating in lonely seas. It can take time to adjust to the lack of a car, the absence of elegant eating places, and all the diversions of home. Many of us have lost the aptitude for stillness and may need a few patient lessons in silence—time to see the Lilliputian landscapes of a forest floor, the patterns of universe in tiny elemental fragments.

I hope this book will appeal both to travelers—the more adventurous sort who enjoy cozy inns and home-style cooking—and to armchair travelers who may never visit these precious places except in their own minds.

Islands are indeed precious. They remind us of alternatives for living, of options, of possibilities, of values often forgotten in the hyped-up pace of modern life. Scores of times I've watched visitors stand enviously on the dockside as lobstermen unload their catch and stroll together to the fishhouses for evenings among the traps and buoys. I've seen "comers-in" on the empty beaches and pine-wood paths, wondering, wishing—wanting.

Islands, however, have their problems, some obvious even to the most casual observer, others deeply hidden in the invisible networks and interrelationships of island people. Most prevalent today are problems of island economies: The lack of employment for the young, declining catches from the ocean, the high cost of island-imports, the high cost of housing due to the inflated prices paid by willing outsiders, and the paucity of many services. The effects threaten the island way of life as we would like to know it. Alcoholism, petty crime, excessive welfare support, and the absence of a new generation of "true" islanders—all can reinforce the declining quality of island life for island residents.

Yet there are notable exceptions. The most promising trend is a balance of old and new life-ways, mainlanders merging with long-time residents to give new life to these ancient places. Adjustments can be difficult, tinged with preconceptions and deep prejudices, but in most of the places I explored, new interrelationships are developing slowly and effectively. The magic of island life and island-living still exists.

Islands are invariably fascinating and mysterious. The "idea" of islands is perhaps more important than the reality. They symbolize independence and individuality; they are places to pursue (and maybe even realize) fantasies and dreams, places to know and understand deeply and totally. Islands are as much states of mind as they are tangible entities. As John Fowles writes in his beautiful little book, *Islands:*

Islands strip and dissolve the crud of our pretensions and cultural accretions.... (They) offer to become a part of all who tread and love them. One returns to the roots of something beyond one's personal descent.

Join me.
And may you enjoy all your journeys.

1. St. Pierre-Miquelon

Fragments of France

Unexpected places. Twelve French-owned islands floating lonely off the Newfoundland coast 190 miles northeast of Nova Scotia; the last rocky remnants of France's once-vast empire stretching from the Gulf of Mexico to Hudson Bay. Only three are of significant size; access is difficult; the weather often appalling; the landscape bleak; the currency and customs unfamiliar, and recreational diversions minimal. Hardy places for hardy travelers.

I came for two good reasons. First, I have a curiosity about isolated, idiosyncratic, difficult-to-reach places. They are usually more vivid and possess more indigenous truth than homogenized resort islands. Generations of interdependence between inhabitants, land, and ocean create a natural harmony that stamps true character on the place. Second, I came for the French food. I came for tartes aux moules, fresh cod baked in Gruyère sauce, halibut with garlic and tarragon, homemade pâtés from island charcuteries, fresh croissants, brioches and baguettes from local boulangeries, the Coquilles St. Jacques, the famed "Vacherin" ice cream cake, and tangy fresh berries picked from the treeless terrain of these islands. And the wines, an excellent range of hard-to-find vintages and regional wines imported duty-free directly from the motherland along with regional cheeses, Périgueux delicacies, and all the tempting trifles found in the great urban markets of France.

First impressions of St. Pierre can be misleading. When I arrived in the tiny town of 5,000 people I seriously questioned the likelihood of cosmopolitan cuisine in such a modest place. Tiers of simple frame and stucco houses rose up the tundra-colored hillside above the wharves. A few overbearing examples of public architecture squatted near the waterfront and in the formal main square, La Place du General de Gaulle, but the high-pitched Basque rooflines somewhat relieved the pomposity of these buildings, and provided a sense of ethnic linkage with the residents' homeland.

Basque and Portuguese fisherman who have plied these shores since the 14th century gave the 100 square miles of islands and islets the collective and descriptive title of "Terra di Bacalaos"—the Land of the Cod. I much prefer the title given by the Portuguese explorer, Joao Alvares Fagundes, who sailed by on October 21, 1520 and named them "The Eleven Thousand Virgins." Somehow the idea of these gray, fog-bound, treeless bits of isolated rock teeming with doe-eyed virgins is totally enchanting, if a little ludicrous. The god-fearing explorer, however, was not celebrating his good fortune but merely recording for posterity the fact that he arrived here on the feast day of St. Ursula, who was martyred in the City of Cologne along with 11,000 virginal supporters sometime around 300 AD. Bit of a let-down there.

After an hour or two sipping fine Beaujolais at St. Pierre's Île de France Hotel (a remarkable restorative after the bumpy flight from Sydney), I strolled the narrow streets dotted with stores and wandered along the cove lined with more simple houses and fish shacks. The true "Frenchness" of the town became evident. Old widows walked as they do in Europe, wrapped entirely in black—black scarf covering most of their head, black coat, black stockings, and black shoes. The street signs were distinctly French and the frenzied tooting and crackling of mopeds and scooters reminded me of the Parisian din. Cars were everywhere—an international diversity of makes and styles. And the colors of the houses! Only the French could create such a visual cacaphony of purple on pink, scarlet on aquamarine, blue on canary yellow, orange on prune. The men, young and old, playing the furious ball games of pétangue and fronton in the square with stolid Basque determination, the smells of fresh-baked bread, the sidewalk cafés complete with "Ricard" signs and customers in black berets and bills paid in French currency, the trilling sound of accordions from the jukeboxes, and even a gendarme dressed in full regalia surreptitiously smoking a Gauloise under the tricolor in the square before the evening "promenade"—all were reminders of France.

I used snippets of my appalling French, much to the amusement of storekeepers. The language spoken here is less harsh than the Quebec dialect and I found it easier to understand. Even the dour fishermen in their berets and blue jackets seemed sympathetic to my modest efforts. Their wind-etched faces tell of thousands of hard days out in "petite pêche" dories, fishing for cod. Many have switched to larger trawlers to meet the challenge of Russian and Japanese fleets that scour the banks and deplete the shoals. The strong-minded, blunt-speaking St. Pierrais resent the intrusions but recognize they have no alternative but to compete as hard as they can.

Still, there are signs of a tranquil side to life. Many homes have small kitchen gardens neatly planted with flowers and vegetables—leeks, onions, beets, parsley, endives, and often a grazing patch for a pet horse. The rich soil

St. Pierre

originally came to the island as ballast on sailing ships from France. Extensive official vacations also provide time for relaxing amusements. August, the traditional French "mois des vacances," is a constant round of parties and picnics, plus the popular Fête de Jacques Cartier on the first Sunday of the month.

When Cartier arrived in 1536 he claimed the islands for France and gave them their current names. Subsequent ownership switched quite regularly. As the great French empire was decimated during the eighteenth and nineteenth centuries, the islands were granted to the British by the Treaty of Utrecht in 1713, returned to France under the Treaty of Paris in 1763, rendered a kind of no-man's-land during the Revolutionary War when the English removed the entire population, and finally were returned to France as a last token of her power, under the Treaty of Versailles, in 1816.

During its history the unfortunate town of St. Pierre has been destroyed on five occasions, twice by war and three times by accident. A particularly severe decimation took place in 1778 when the English purposely torched the town after expelling the inhabitants. St. Pierre remained a mess of crumbled homes and broken docks for years. Everything had to be rebuilt after the war, but the hardy Bretons, Normans, and Basques soon had the economy booming again with bounteous hauls of cod from the Newfoundland Banks.

Smuggling was a popular sub-economy and the St. Pierrais became true masters of the art during Prohibition in the nineteen-twenties. Sailing ships, fishing trawlers, and even tiny dories plied the long rough route between St. Pierre and major east coast cities, delivering millions of gallons of illicit liquor. Enormous warehouses were built below the bare slopes of "the mountain" which rises up steeply behind the town, and even the naval barracks were used as overspill storage areas during the height of "La Fraude." Rum-runners were respected members of the local community and the sudden glut of new tax monies enabled town fathers to create a "model" community of imposing public buildings, monuments, and memorials to just about every significant French hero since the middle ages.

The "Temps de la Fraude" ended officially in 1935 by decree of the French government in Paris, under pressure from the U.S. and Canadian administrations. Nevertheless, differences in the liquor prices between the Canadian mainland and St. Pierre, encouraged a more modest trade for many more years. Fisherman-smugglers invented ingenious methods to avoid prosecution by patrol boats, the most effective of which was to enclose liquor bottles in bags of rock salt and cork. As "mounties" approached, the bags would be thrown overboard and sunk. Within a couple of days the salt would dissolve and the bags float back up to the surface buoyed by the cork, ready for reclamation. Subsequently light planes and very high speed boats were also used but today the trade is virtually extinct (so I was informed).

A more legitimate diversion here during the warm months is a day trip by dory to the outer islands across the dangerous four mile strait from St. Pierre, the "Gueuie d'Enfer"—the "Mouth of Hell." Particularly dramatic is the high plateau of Langdale tied to the larger island, Miquelon, by a flat sandy isthmus known as "La Dune." The rocky shoals, 500 foot high cliffs and deceptive shallows have wrecked over 600 ships in the last century. Yet Langdale itself is a pleasantly wooded place notched by narrow dark valleys, ideal for family picnicking or afternoons of rabbit and deer hunting. The few scattered farms that exist are marginal affairs. Fewer than 60 people live here permanently, augmenting their subsistence economy by fishing and collecting driftwood from the beaches.

Miquelon to the north is a bleaker place, over 80 square miles of low bare hills known as "mornes", an appropriately dismal-sounding name for this barren landscape of moors, peat bogs, and thin brown streams. Wild ponies roam the hills, about 60 at last count. The southern portion of the island consists mainly of a salt water lagoon, the Grand Barachois, edged by dunes and linked to the ocean by a narrow channel. Gray seals frolic here in the summer, but in the winter it is often smothered in dense fog or broken into high waves by the fierce "poudrin" winds that tear across the wastes at speeds exceeding 100 miles an hour.

Almost 600 people live in the village of Miquelon which, like many northern French villages, consists of two long rows of houses and little flower-filled gardens facing one another across a main street. Many of the newer houses are built of concrete and even attempts to give them a clapboard finish cannot soften their austere appearance. Horses, cattle, and sheep roam in the moist meadows and dunes surrounding the community.

Access from St. Pierre is often difficult for newcomers; it took me almost a whole morning to discover the time and location of the ferry for the four-mile crossing. And there's little to do when you arrive except stroll around the salt pans, read the inscriptions on the cemetery headstones, exchange greetings with residents who rarely seem to leave their homes, avoid the semi-wild dogs, and wait for food at Pension Touristique de Georges Cox.

The lunch, Boeuf Bourguignon with tiny potatoes, endive salad, and a

The Dories of St. Pierre
— one of the most
beautiful boats

light mousse made from a puree of fresh-picked cloudberries with cream, was excellent. But I was glad to return to the "metropolis" of St. Pierre, back to the Place de la Liberté, La Rue du Maréchal Foch, La Rue Sadi Carnot, and the descriptive L'Avenue de l'Abattoir. You feel at home again among the tooting scooters and the alert prickliness of the residents.

Length of stay here depends on your appetite and your fascination with such small attractions as the historical museum behind the hospital, the preponderance of memorials, monuments and statues, the lines of high-prowed dories along the strand by the "salines" (fishermen's huts), and, my favorite place, the cemetery above the town where, because of the rocky ground, graves are partially raised and kept pristine white and bedecked with flowers in typical European fashion.

Keep an alert eye open for little oddities. Beyond the power plant, for example, is an imitation of the grotto in Lourdes where Bernadette had her miraculous vision, and nearby, along Boulevard Thelot, is a tiny waterfall surrounded by an iron fence commemorating the spot where the famous French writer and philosopher, René de Chateaubriand, dallied with a St. Pierre girl in 1791.

The community is full of such little surprises, although I expected more evidence of an Acadian culture—memorials to the sad Evangeline and the like. Statues of the Virgin Mary are everywhere, but Evangeline gets short shrift. The Basque heritage is, however, very evident at Place Richard Briand with its pélota court and the proud nationalistic statement scrawled on a nearby wall—"Zazpiak Bat"—"The Seven are One", referring to the seven Pyrenees provinces of the traditional Basque nation which overlap the French/Spanish border.

Away from the town the bleak landscape asserts itself. There is always wind, often with a chill Labradorean edge. Fogs, caused by the nearby confluence of the warm Gulf Stream and the cold Baffin current, move in quickly off the ocean. Rocks, peat bogs, and small farms punctuate the slopes of the mountain behind the town. Only on the western lee side can one find trees of any size, little swathes of stunted woodlands shaped by the wind. There are lonely walks up here and excellent places for bird watching, but once again, it's comforting to return to the pensions and restaurants of the town.

The Île de France and Hotel Robert are among the best hotels but perfectly adequate accommodation can be found at such pensions as Chez Madame Henri Vigneau, Chez Roland Vigneau and Marcel Helene's, where the lively owner Jeanne, typically French to her sandalled feet, keeps her guests in a constant state of amusement.

"Well—are you enjoying your stay on our little island?" Jeanne asked me with a bequiling smile.

I patted my stomach and hiccuped.

She patted my stomach too. "Ah yes—a typical Pierrais tummy. Full and round."

I was tempted to return the gesture but hiccuped again instead.

Her husband nodded knowingly from his armchair.

Among the restaurants, Madame Josephine Dutin's "Chez Dutin" is one of the best for simple, inexpensive meals. I enjoyed an excellent lunch of Artichauts à la Mazarin, Asperges en sauce mousseline, Poulet farci avec pommes braiseés, salade, Gateau Normande, coffee, and two house wines, a dry Blanc de Blanc and a fruity Côtes-du-Rhone—all for a modest $9 (and a kiss on the cheek from the waitress). Other places well worth sampling are the Caveau (an appropriately dark bistro), Chez Gegene, La Cascade, and the ornate Joinville.

Also, if you have chance, get an invitation to one of the island homes. The exterior may need a new paint job (the high winds and salt spray wear down even the toughest exterior paints, often exposing shingles made from old whisky crates during "La Fraude"!) but the interior will be spotless. Furnishings are simple and the largest room is usually the kitchen where windows are sealed tight in the winter against the penetrating *poudrin* winds. Small porches known locally as "tambours" protect doorways against snow, and everywhere during the cold dark months you'll find flowers and potted plants as reminders of spring-time.

And finally when the fine food and the stores offering cut-price wines and French luxuries (Albert Briand's store is one of the best) begin to pall, find a boat to one of the tiny off-islands and regain that sense of utter solitude that attracts travelers here.

Seamen's Island (L'Île aux Marins) is a short float across St. Pierre's harbor and was a summer home for foreign fishermen a few decades ago. The low rocky shoreline was once carpeted by split cod drying in the sun during the warm season. Now the place is uninhabited, with remnants of simple houses and a wooden church. It's an excellent spot to watch passing whales or small icebergs, during the spring thaw.

Most of the other islets are rocky outcrops populated by terns and gulls. Grand Colombier, off the northern tip of St. Pierre Island, is a particularly barren place of towering cliffs topped by a little fresh water tarn fed by fogs and rains. A tribe of large voracious rats is said to inhabit this place, feasting on eggs and young birds during the April-September nesting season—not a very pleasant sight according to local fishermen.

The future for St. Pierre-Miquelon seems bright. Cruise ships are making regular stops here now that the harbor is a safer place to dock, and talk of off-shore oil keeps the French government interested in these tiny bits of rock and the welfare of their inhabitants (to the tune of $5 million of economic support annually). New ideas for island development constantly amuse the somewhat sceptical populace—elaborate schemes for casinos, huge international duty-free port facilities, the creation of a breeding center for enormous 3,000 pound Charolais cattle, and the development of a "showcase" for French culture and French products.

Meanwhile life continues rather languorously with pétangue games behind the pelota court, wine-sipping in the cafes, cod-fishing on the banks when the shoals are sighted, and long damp days in mists and fogs. Changes may come, but they will tend to come slowly in this bastion of Basque and Breton culture. The people will not easily give up their heritage, their traditions, and their slow-paced approach to life. And why should they? The world needs more places like St. Pierre-Miquelon.

2. The Magdalen Islands

Acadia in the Gulf of St. Lawrence

One early September morning I sat on a fat dune peering out over twenty miles of empty sandhills and broad cream beaches. Breezes with a tang of sea-spray blew through the marram grass and a string of cormorants skimmed the wavelets like shadows. In the far distance tiny white cottages lay scattered daisy-fashion across the green hills of Grosse Île; the Lagune de la Grande Entrée was a sheet of silver reflecting fishing boats, canneries, and herring smokehouses along the waterfront of Grand Entrée village.

My stomach rumbled with the pleasure of it all and memories of last night's bouillabaise at La Table des Roy restaurant in La Vernière. Typically, I'd eaten far too much of the rich saffron and fennel-flavored stock brimming with lobster and scallops and my anatomy still protested, an anatomy which two days previously had been subjected to such onslaughts that I wondered if I'd ever eat again.

A Micmac Indian on Prince Edward Island was to blame. While rambling the quiet western byways of that peaceful island, luxuriating in cozy red sandstone coves and talking with local fishermen, I met a well-traveled Indian from the Lenox Island reservation who described his recent journey to the Magdalen Islands, a hundred miles or so north in the Gulf of St. Lawrence. He talked about the hospitality he'd received from the Acadian-French population, the traditional "Pot-en-pot" seafood casseroles, the miles of empty beaches, and inexpensive accommodation in the homes of "Madelinot" islanders.

Curiosity prevailed and next day I boarded the 2 p.m. ferry from Souris on Prince Edward Island. Regrettably, my grasp of French is limited and warnings over the ferry intercom went ignored although I wondered at the time why I was only one of three people enjoying a late lunch in the dining room. A few minutes after dessert the tail of some riproaring hurricane wagged its way directly across our path and for the next four hours and 32 minutes we were tossed like rubber ducks in a baby's bath. Bodies lay everywhere clutching table tops and sofa legs. I closed my eyes and died frequently.

Frederic Landry supervised my convalescence. This unusual man—priest,

Baraques
on the Magdalens

boat-captain, radio celebrity, historian, and author—is also director of the Musee de la Mer in Havre-Aubert at the southern tip of the Magdalens. With typical Acadian kindness he hosted me at his harborside home and ensured my recovery with bowls of fresh clams cooked in their own broth, thick chunks of home-baked bread, slices of smoked herring from the museum's own miniature smokehouse, and glass after glass of sturdy Quebec burgundy.

Next day I was up and frisky, out exploring the seven islands of the main Magdalen archipelago all linked by thin tendrils of dunes. Each island has its little mountains, the last writhings of America's great Appalachian system. Young fir forests cover much of Grindstone and Amherst islands; the others are virtually treeless and the random scatterings of small cottages are reminiscent of the Scottish Hebrides. Many of these homes are charmingly Victorian, graced by high-pitched gables and "carpenter-gothic" trim.

With the exception of two small clusters of English-speaking families at Grosse Île and Entry Island out in Pleasant Bay, the majority of the 15,000 Madelinots are of Acadian descent and still maintain a fierce loyalty to their sad history so movingly captured in Longfellow's "Evangeline".

Prior to the American Revolution, French settlers, mainly from Brittany and Normandy, flourished as farmers and fishermen in the English colony of "Acadia", formed from a portion of Nova Scotia in 1713. As colonial friction increased between France and England the presence of a substantial French-speaking minority in the colony was considered dangerous. Acadians who refused to swear oaths of allegiance were forcibly deported in the "Grand Dérangement" of 1755. Families were splintered; some fled south to the lower colonies of Virginia and Carolina and most notably to the bayous of Louisiana where they retained their distinct "Cajun" culture. A few settled in the Magdalen Islands, only to be scattered again or subjected to feudal control by new English landowners during the late 18th century. It was not until 1895 that Acadian Madelinots were finally allowed to purchase land and build an independent economy on the islands, free of colonial domination.

Now, as part of the State of Quebec, the islanders enthusiastically retain their French heritage. While lacking some of the duty-free extravagances of St. Pierre-Miquelon, 200 miles to the north east, they live and eat well on the ocean's bounties. Lobsters, scallops, herring, cod, mackerel, and crabs are all found abundantly in nearby waters; the fishing villages of Étang-du-Nord, Havre-Aubert and Grand-Entrée are bright with gaudy boats and redolent with the aromas of herring smokehouses and canneries (usually open to the public during the summer).

Island restaurants offer seafood in all guises. The tiny blue Maison de la Couline, overlooking the ocean at Bassin, is best-known for its famous Acadian Pot-en-Pot dinners featuring layers of seafood separated by sliced potatoes and onions cooked casserole-style in rich broth, topped with a pastry crust. The Auberge de la Jetée, near the ferry terminal in Cap-aux-Meules, offers a wider range of simply-prepared seafood creations in a setting of Victorian elegance. There's also the cosy La Table des Roy at La Vernière with a handful of tables and plump Francine Roy supervising the preparation of her delicate hors d'oeuvres of Pétoncles Marines (scallops marinated in lemon juice and served in thin raw slices with flower-patterned garnishes), fresh mussels in white wine, prawns in white sauce with puff pastry, and her far-too-generous Bouillabaise full of sea food and complete with fiery rouille and croutons. Light-as-a-cloud maple soufflé is a wicked way to end a memorable dinner here.

Of course, you could forget the big dinner for a day and concentrate on island snacks: thin strips of pungent smoked herring washed down with beer, slices of rich pâté de la Campagne, available in local stores with a bottle of strong French cider, lobster rolls bursting with cold cooked lobster, fresh clams and mussels, a score of different fish chowders and bisques and—for meat lovers—slices of Acadian meat pie made with strips of pork and beef between crisp pastry crusts.

Then come the quiet explorations of these sea-wrapped islets. Drive, bike, or walk up the Butte du Vent in the center of Grindstone Island for the best views over the whole archipelago. Travel to Pointe de l'Est at the northern tip, which was recently declared a National Wildlife Area famous for its unspoiled marine environment. Migratory birds pause here by the tens of thousands during the fall and you can lose yourself for a day on the wriggling paths between the dunes. No vehicles penetrate the wilderness; the world belongs to you. And that's part of the magic of the Magdalens. During the summer hundreds of adventure-starved travelers are quickly absorbed. You can walk the sand-ribbons between the islands and claim miles of beach as your own. The great North Dune between Grosse Île and Grindstone Island is over 23 miles long and the even more isolated West Dune, while a mere eight miles long, is one of the loneliest walks I've ever experienced—just the sand, the sea, and long, long silences. Be sure you enjoy your own company before trying this one.

For the more gregarious visitor there are fishing trips out into the Gulf of St.

Cliffs. Cap-aux-Meules

Lawrence, pedallo boats for two at the northern end of Cap-aux-Meules, Grand-Entreé's eat-all-you-can lobster festival on the first weekend in June and the Fishermen's Festival the following weekend, an Acadian festival usually in mid-August, and the excellent island museum and the Madelinot village at Havre-Aubert. I spent an afternoon here browsing through restored cottages, craft shops, smokehouses and a cannery, then adjourned to the Café de la Grave in the old general store across the road for a bowl of homemade cream of celery soup, served to the accompaniment of an impromptu Mozart piano recital by one of the waitresses.

There's one adventure that many visitors overlook. Tiny Entry Island out in Pleasant Bay is home for a handful of families descended from Scottish settlers and stranded victims of shipwrecks whose vessels once floundered by the score on the sandbars and shoals of the Magdalens. The islanders here speak a curious kind of dialect tinged with Scottish phrases. Their houses seem even smaller and cozier than the ones on the main islands and while the people are friendly to newcomers, they obviously relish their semi-isolation on the green slopes of the island's 599 foot peak, the highest point in the archipelago. Paths leading to the eastern side of the island end in abrupt red cliffs laced with caves and alive with cormorants. The village side consists of a gently tilting plateau leading down to a tight rocky harbor.

If you left the car behind in Souris on Prince Edward Island (the ferry fee is high and delays can be exasperating if you insist on bringing one) you can hire another in Cap-aux-Meules or better still, rent a bike and explore the winding backroads of Grindstone and Amherst Islands. The archipelago is less than 50 miles from end to end, so everything is easily accessible. Scattered, like the tiny houses, are the unusual Magdalen "baraques" used for hay storage. The challenge was to design a structure that required little wood, was flexible in height, gave easy access and good ventilation to the hay, and had a roof for protection and for securing hay during occasionally-fierce storms. The resulting semi-open box with a pitched roof that can be raised to hold varied amounts of hay is a brilliant piece of folk-engineering and an admirable photographic subject.

Because of the exposed location of the islands and the absence of trees, the wind here is a notable shaper of island character. The strips of dunes constantly change form and size after winter storms; the tall red sandstone cliffs, particularly at Étang du Nord and Old Harry, have been hollowed, chiseled, and smoothed by the ferocious pounding of wind-whipped surf. Many of the cottages have little wind-porches protecting the front door, and even the impressive new Catholic churches at Fatima and La Vernière have been streamlined to reduce the impact of wind on their broad roof-spans. During the long winters the winds become truly ferocious, blowing snow into 20 foot high drifts in places and freezing the ocean in Pleasant Bay to such thickness that islanders make skidoo trips across the ice to Entry Island, over 12 miles from Cap-aux-Meules.

Before regular air and sea ferries, the Magdalens were notoriously isolated during the cold months. In the particularly vicious winter of 1910 the islanders felt so marooned on their tiny bastion of frozen sand and sea that they protested to the world by filling a wooden barrel with complaints to government officials, equipping it with sail and rudder and setting it adrift in the open waters of the Gulf. Four weeks later the famous "ponchon" bumped ashore on Cape Breton Island and created such public outcry that the embarrassed government in Ottawa dispatched special ice-breaking supply ships and wireless communication equipment in an unprecedented burst of efficiency

Even today's regular links with the outside world have left much of the island way of life untouched. Homes are still modestly furnished; the Acadian-French population enjoys its own folk music, and sees little need to learn English; baraques are still regarded as the best way of storing hay, and Aucoin, Leblanc, Gaudet, Poirier, and Décoste remain the most familiar names on Amherst and Grindstone islands.

The 700 Scottish descendents around Grosse Île are equally nationalistic. They hold down their hay in Hebridean fashion with rock-weighted nets, worship at their New England-styled Anglican chapel in Old Harry, eat fish and chips and sausage and mash at Kerry's Country Kitchen, and enjoy English-language movies at the Strand cinema on the edge of a small lagoon near the new salt mine.

The Magdalens are not for the heavy-action tourist anxious to plan vacation days as tightly as office schedules. The pleasure comes from the silences, the long dune walks, the seafood dinners in cozy guest houses and restaurants. Like the St. Pierrais, the Madelinots have enjoyed over two centuries of simple living and proud independence, and it will take far more than a few summer tourists to change all that.

3. Grand Manan

A Strong and Lonely Place

Scene: Eight years ago; West Quoddy Head at the northern tip of Maine; a misty drizzling day. On the horizon a ball of black cumulus sat directly over an island, a strong and lonely place. Shafts of sun turned the bulk into patchworks of bright greens and bronzes. Cliffs rose hundreds of feet from the surf line to fir-topped crags. No houses, no smoke, no boats, none of the dainty accoutrements of islands further to the south—just cliffs, forests, clouds and ocean.

The island was Grand Manan, the southern outpost of Canada, accessible only from the Canadian side of Passamaquoddy Bay. Eight years ago I passed up the chance to go; this time I made it.

Perhaps, though, I should start by emphasizing the reasons for not coming. There are the summer mosquitoes and black flies—real biters. There are the fogs which in typical Fundy-fashion can lie like limp pancakes over the island for days. Then there are those summertime waits for the lethargic ferry at a spot without stores, hotels, and people. Add to this the ban on liquor at the island hotels and restaurants, no evening entertainment, the virtual absence of non-reserved accommodation during peak season, a scarcity of good beaches, an ocean usually too cold for swimming, and you have pretty good justification for considering the Bahamas instead. Even the normally placid Champlain thought it was a "miserable place" when he lost an anchor in a Fundy storm here in 1606.

If too many people decided to withstand all these very real shortcomings, Grand Manan could quickly lose the magical properties that bring her admirers back year after year. Willa Cather was one of the island's most celebrated visitors. During the thirties she spent many summers here with her companion Edith Lewis, in a cottage hidden behind trees at Whale Cove. Lewis wrote: "Willa found the island so simple and primitive in all the conditions of living, a great resource, an increasingly congenial place to work...the beautiful silence, accentuated instead of diminished by the sound of the sea on the shingle, the wind blowing the elder bushes, the songs of hundreds of birds, was tranquillizing to the spirit and seemed to open up great spaces for it to roam in."

The
Great
Cliffs of
Grand
Manan.

I felt the change as soon as I arrived after a calm two hour, 20 mile crossing spent in the sun watching the great basalt cliffs rear out of the bay. Within minutes I was a welcome guest at the Compass Rose in North Head village, a tiny shore-side hotel with cozy doll's house bedrooms, a small dining room full of fresh flowers, a terrace overlooking the harbor, and a very reasonable price tag for a single room with breakfast.

Lunch came, beginning with a bowl of fresh fish chowder and a small homebaked wholewheat loaf. I talked with a dapper gentleman who, after 40 years of summer residence, still bubbled with enthusiasm for the island. It turned out his daughter was one of the hotel's owners and he had just celebrated his 91st birthday. Then the Coquille St. Jacques arrived, a generous helping of melt-in-the-mouth scallops basking in a rich vermouth sauce accompanied by a salad flecked with dulse, Grand Manan's famous edible seaweed.

Looking south from the terrace across Long Island Bay's spindling fishing-weirs with such defeatist names as No Good, Try Again, and Hard Luck, I could see the dark green fir forests which cover most of the island's fifty or so square miles. From the eastern shoreline, cut with coves and protected by scatterings of tiny islets, Grand Manan tilts upwards towards the 400 foot basalt cliffs of its western edge rising like battlements from the ocean. What paved roads there are follow the 15 mile long eastern shore from the small lighthouse at Northern Head. Only one dirt road cuts a four mile link across the island to the sandbar-protected cove of Dark Harbor, center of the island's dulse harvesting. Here a handful of fishermen spend the summer months dragging thick ribbons of purple seaweed ashore and drying them on nets along the rocky beach. The drying process cannot be rushed, so much of the time is passed paying social six-pack calls among the lopsided tarpaper cabins above the high tide mark. Before sunset the mats of dulse are rolled and taken off in trucks for packaging as an edible snack and salad-booster, or for grinding into powder used for pharmaceutical and flavoring purposes.

It's a pleasant, diverting kind of summer occupation when the herring fishing is poor, as it has been for the last few years. Promising though are the aquaculture experiments for salmon-breeding out in the harbor. The project is only a couple of years old but already Japanese orders make it appear a winner.

Highlights of the coastal drive alongside the bays and coves of the eastern shore are the picturesque groupings of shacks, herring smokehouses, and old canneries at North Head, Woodward's Cove and, most notably, the village of Seal Cove. If you have even the remotest urge to paint or take photographs then you'll come to know this place well and spend hours exploring the twisted wharves, empty warehouses, and narrow alleys smelling of lobsters and tar.

On the hill above the harbor sit the twin bastions of this tight-knit community, the Baptist and Wesleyan churches. Religion is no casual matter on Grand Manan. For a resident population of 2,500, many of them descendents of 18th century Loyalist settlers who came to escape the purges of the American Revolution, the island has 15 churches. Most recreational and social activities are church-related. One elderly lady told me: "Everyone knows what you're doing any time day or night. You either live celibate or you have a reputation." A younger man who claimed he "couldn't quite get the hang of fishing" and spent much of his time seeking out psychedelic mushrooms in the woods at Northern Point, said bluntly that "half the islanders are alcoholics and the other half pray for 'em."

Certainly alcohol has created a few problems here. Many of the traditional families—the Ingalls, Greens, Browns, Guptills and Daggets ("you can tell which name a fella's got, just from lookin' at him") disagreed about the opening of a State Liquor store on the island in 1972. Now people can drink in private but the diehards are determined to prevent public drinking in bars or hotels. "They won't even let guests have wine with dinner," I was told by one hotel-owner. "But we have our little ways. After all, whoever said teapots were made just for tea...."

Gleason Green thinks there are more important concerns than liquor, such as the recent absence of herring around the islands. "There was a time boat'd come back after haulin' and they'd be full of herrin', tumblin' over the side they'd be, enough to keep a hundred smokehouses on the go." For reasons unknown the herring have become elusive, leaving island fisherman relying on lobsters and scallops for their livelihood. "Lobster's are fine. More than enough for everybody. You can make a good livin' here off lobsters and scallops. I've still got the record though—when I was 76 I brought the biggest catch ever come into this island in one day—3,600 pounds—I hauled a little under 300 traps and sold 'em at $3.30 a pound. Calculate that out for a day's work! There's some fellas on here that got to be millionaires. I ain't one of 'em but I can keep alright."

Seal Cove · Grand
Manan

Gleason Green is a true "character." At 85 he lives by himself in a house close to his sheds on the bay. He possesses , in addition to notoriety as a lobsterman, a reputation as a boat-builder, a craftsman, a green-thumb gardener, a passable cook, an inventor, a raconteur and an enthusiastic traveler. "Went to Norway a couple of years back. Now I'm wondering about India. Always been curious about India. Or Australia...." He paused and squashed a bug on his pants. "Danged things. I been out in the potatoes. Y'see that patch over there, past the cabbages. I got 15 sacks off that this year—all from one potato I snuck back from Norway. Customs went through everything to find seeds. They missed the potato. It was in m' pocket."

I wondered if he ever tired of fishing.

"Never. Never missed a year yet. When my son gets his boat loaded to go out I take the wheel just as she's mine and go set the traps where I want to. Then last thing at night when you're comin' in you get the fire goin' just before you get done haulin', boil up a pot of seawater and chuck three or four lobsters on the stove. Few minutes'll do. Let 'em cool a bit and take 'em down with butter. Nothin' like it. Nothin' I've ever eaten."

Strolling around his vegetable patch he showed me a modified wheelbarrow he'd invented. "Seems like it works. I got orders for 8 more like this. People are always comin' to see what I'm makin', some of them I used to take on trips around the islands 20 years back."

I asked what he considered to be the island's highlights and, quick as a back-paddling lobster, he rattled off a complete itinerary which I used for my own explorations.

I began at Southern Head, bouncing along a dusty earth track winding through pine forests. A footpath led up past the lighthouse to the abrupt cliff edge where thousands of broken basalt colums rise like organ pipes from the surf 300 feet below. Fingal's Cave and Giant's Causeway all rolled into one.

You can stroll north for a mile or two along a cliff-top path that dips into woods littered with wild strawberries. There are also paths down to tight little coves, but the climb back can be wearing. Nine miles out is the Gannet Rock lighthouse, a welcome guide through the treacherous Fundy shoals, manned by two keepers who keep lonely month-long vigils.

To the east are dozens of islets, some mere rocky outcrops, others more substantial like White Head Island reached by a free ferry (every two hours) from Ingall's Head. I spent a day here exploring the white basalt coves and talking with the smokehouse men. The aroma of smoldering spruce sawdust rolls along the narrow village street between neat shingle homes. Each smokehouse contains 100 hogsheads of herring, tens of thousands of fish skewered on wooden rods slowly changing color from blue-gray to bright bronze over a six week period. Afterwards the women of the village fillet and skin the fish and pack them into ten pound boxes for export to the West Indies. This trade goes back to the days when herring strips were valuable barter for West Indian rum.

If you'd like to see the outer islands, particularly Kent and Machias Seal Islands with their colonies of rare birds—arctic terns, razorbills, petrels, puffins and auks—ask any islander where to find Preston Wilcox, a very experienced boatman. Of course you may feel even more adventurous and want to go sailing with island fishermen (ask nicely) or, better still, join special whale-watching trips led by Dr. David Gaskin. Headquarters for these expeditions is Jim and Fern Leslie's magnificent Marathon Inn, an ornately mansarded masterpiece of Victoriana perched high on the hillside overlooking North Head Village. Accommodation here consists of 36 rooms (delightfully furnished with antiques, painted wood beds and dressers), two museum-like lounges, huge fireplaces, refined dining room, and film room. Here Dr. Gaskin makes his presentations on the lifestyles of North Atlantic Right whales and then leads enthusiastic groups laden with cameras and binoculars far out into the bay to watch the surfacings from a forty foot fishing boat or, for the truly courageous, a tiny inflated dinghy.

If all this sounds a little too active, there's always the museum at Grand Harbor village where over 300 stuffed island birds can be viewed at leisure. Grand Manan was a favorite spot of James Audubon who visited here in 1832 and recorded over 250 different species of birds, including the bald eagle which still nests on the island. Other excellent displays here include a description of island history and fishing methods, geological exhibits, and the old lens from the Gannet lighthouse, an enormous ten foot creature of curved polished glass prisms.

Best of all, though, on warm summer days, are the secluded beaches at the Anchorage Camping Park, Red Point with its magnetic sands and unusual rock formations, Castalia (a favorite with residents), and Whale Cove.

Towards the end of my stay I spent a quiet afternoon at the cove. A few "dulsers" were there also, sipping their beers and waiting for the seaweed to dry. On the eastern edge of the cove, in a worn cliff full of surf-made incisions, was the "Hole in the Wall" cave, accessible by footpath from the Marathon

Rolling in
the
Dulse
— Grand
Manan

Inn. A little to the east sat the dainty lighthouse at Swallow Tail, reached by precarious footbridge. Behind me, peering through trees, was the cottage where Willa Cather spent contented summers writing her novels.

Eric Allaby, curator of the museum and a prominent islander, told me that with all the ferry delays and other difficulties, "you really have to want to come here." He's right, but if you do come, may your spirit, like Willa Cather's, find those "great spaces to roam in."

4. Deer Island

A Dainty Detour

From Eastport in Maine or Canada's Campobello Island (FDR's "beloved island") ferries run regularly throughout the summer to the southern tip of this charming backwater islet in Passamaquoddy Bay. The journey saves at least 50 road miles and is a far more enticing way of reaching the Grand Manan ferry at Black's Harbor.

On the crossing watch out for Old Sow, claimed to be the world's largest whirlpool. The remarkable Bay of Fundy tides, reaching summer highs of up to 40 feet, create a series of vicious swirls and eddies which grunt and gurgle with all the abandon of a hungry porker.

After clearing Canadian customs on Deer Island, meander north through deep forests broken by views over coves filled with fishing boats and lopsided piers. The place is quaintly old-fashioned. Demure Victorian homes with all the trimmings sit on primped lawns shaded by oaks and chestnuts. Artists and photographers relish the worn fishing shacks, the coy churches, the rocky inlets edged by fishing weirs and furred with thick seaweed clusters at low tide.

It's not really big enough for a prolonged stay. Stores are few and overnight accommodation is limited to a guest house and motel. So just wander at will for a few hours, taking backroads to the lobster pounds on the west side of the island (the world's largest, holding over 700,000 lbs of lobsters); stroll the dark brown sands of Chocolate Cove, and munch on Sarah Calder's delicious homemade pies and cookies from her bakery in Fairhaven.

Then at Lambertville, near the islands northern tip, catch the free ferry (every ½ hour all year round) and enjoy the wriggling route to Letete past a score of fir-topped islets. This is one of the best little boat trips on the eastern coast of America. Herons stand stick-still in the shallows, occasional porpoise and seals frolic by, and cormorants perch in somber black robes on outcrops.

Twenty minutes in unspoiled limbo—and free too.

Victorian details
on Deer Island

5. Great and Little Cranberry

The Long, Calm Silences

Sneaky places, these Maine islands. They make you restless in the big city; all the scamper of metropolitan life can seem suddenly rather pointless. They creep back quietly as little mind-movies: Lobstermen around a stove in the fishhouse with all the time in the world to talk of island things; slack lines of paths among the black blankets of spruce; the snapping dawn air; a scythe moon above granite ledges, and fresh chowder from clams you raked yourself in a cove on that last island evening. Most of all you remember the long, calm silences when the poet inside beat down the pragmatist, when the real islander inside became part of the solitude. A sense of coming home again.

Wilfred Bunker eases his Sea Queen mailboat out of the dock at Northeast Harbor on Mt. Desert Island and heads down-channel into a frisky ocean. We pass between Bear Island and Greening Island where British sloops were repulsed by the American militia in 1784, past the osprey nests on Sutton Island, and the house where Rachel Field wrote "Time Out of Mind" in the late thirties, and make a bee-line for the jetty on Great Cranberry Island. We leave behind the somnolent cone of Cadillac Mountain, the bare-topped bastion of Mount Desert Island, and the Acadia National Park.

Curious travelers ply Wilfred with questions. He's a patient Yankee gentleman dressed in the traditional Maine outfit of plaid shirt, olive drabs, and baseball cap. His replies are short and there's a twinkle in his eys as he nudges his little boat against the dock and reminds passengers that this is only a four-hour stopover. Along with generations of Fernalds, Stanleys, and Spurlings, the Bunkers have been a part of the Cranberries since 1762 and the company of Beal and Bunker has a benevolent monopoly on island trade. Wilfred knows just about everything worth knowing but shares it sparingly.

It's always quiet here. Main street rises from the pebbly beach to a cluster of elegant Victorian homes. An elderly man with a summer-bronzed face adds

Carl Nelson
—Little Cranberry—

yet one more coat of white paint to a filigree of carpenter-gothic trim and smiles benignly on the straggle of newcomers. Shade trees shroud smaller clapboard cottages. Head-high piles of lobster traps, broken buoys, and coils of stained rope stiff with sea salt fill front yards behind the deer-fences. It's still early morning and the smell of frying bacon hangs under the sycamores.

"Route 1", the island's only road, is a two mile track leading from the jetty to Dolly Hill and Deadman Point at the bottom end of the island where, if you're lucky, you'll catch a glimpse of a rare Leach's Petrel. You can bring (or rent) a bike or adopt a more spontaneous foot-based itinerary, taking side paths at random into deep woods along the western side. Some lead through to little coves and ledges of volcanic breccia and tuff; others end abruptly in the yards of secluded homes peeping between buttresses of cordwood. The 90 or so year-round residents take their wood-cutting seriously, starting early in the year to ensure "good dryin' time" before the long chill sets in.

Paths on the eastern side of Route 1 lead down to The Pool, a placid oval of seawater enveloped by long sandy arms and linked to the ocean by a narrow channel. High gangly piers are indicative of the tidal variations here and a few lopsided sheds are all that remain of the boat-building yards. Apple orchards, overgrown and long-abandoned, fringe the pool and in the fall you'll find the sweetest, crispest little apples in the whole of New England.

"Help yourself. They'll be no good in a week." The laugh-wrinkled face of Carl Nelson peered out from long tresses of white hair and beard. "Wasps get to 'em and they dry up in no time." Along with John Heliker, Robert Lattotan, Lou Wadsworth, and others, Carl is part of Great Cranberry's artist community, a group of individuals who have enjoyed the peace of the island for a dozen years and more. Carl is usually the most visible, a happy guru living in his white and green home half way down Route 1, always out with his cane, smiling at everyone, full of fun.

"The best walk if you've a mind is from the town landing, round the western edges, all the way to Rice Point and the pink boulders," Carl told me. I explained I only had a few hours before the next ferry to Little Cranberry, so he sent me instead looking for the Cranberry Club, a tiny cottage in the woods near Deadman Point. Here, on special occasions throughout the summer, he explained with mock reverence, gathered the social cream of Bar Harbor's female dowagers, representatives of the all-powerful families of old wealth. I wondered what they did when they got there and he made a few imaginative suggestions. Unfortunately I never found the cottage.

Forest has reclaimed much of the lower part of the island which once boasted extensive hayfields, gardens, and the best island Cranberry bog in Maine. The bog was drained in the 1920s in an effort to eliminate mosquitoes. The mosquitoes survived but the cranberries vanished for good.

I got lost in the forest a couple of times, out-stared two deer blocking my path, and arrived back on Route 1 a little breathless. I was lucky. A beat-up Ford truck with no bonnet, no fenders, no lights and no side windows rumbled out of the woods and I got a lift back up the island to the town landing. Carl was still out, sunning himself on his front lawn and holding court with two young visitors. We passed the new library, the white church, the cottage with the rusty anchor, big as an ox, in the front yard, and the mansions on top of the hill. Wilfred's ferry was coming across from Sutton Island trailed by gulls. I sat on a sandy part of the curved beach looking toward the sweep of Cadillac Mountain until he arrived. Then off we skipped across the waves again towards Little Cranberry. A storm was forecast for the evening but I had total faith in Wilfred. "Missed only three days in forty-two years," he told me in his quiet voice. "Takes a lot to stop this boat." Hardly surprising. It was built by his brother.

Little Cranberry feels different, more open, less hemmed in by dark forests. Islesford, the only community, has a sedate Vermont village look complete with broad shade trees, open lawns, spired churches, and neat white and green cottages. Only piles of lobster traps and brightly painted buoys in front yards are reminders of its nautical heritage.

Past the Sawtelle museum, full of old maps, photographs, and memorabilia of the region, I paused in the pleasantly musty general store and bought a copy of Ted Spurling's island guide and a hiker's map. The dusty street passed the chapel and the school and turned south toward the beach. The woods closed in briefly with a smell of warm resin. Crickets hummed the afternoon away in the underbrush; I could see the surf and hear the constant grinding of beach pebbles.

The rocky beach curved out to the old coast guard station at Bar Point. At last—the open Atlantic. From so many of Maine's islands all you see are more islands. But here is wide water, sapphire blue and still, under cottonball clouds. Resilient hikers brag of long hard walks around the point and up to

Little Cranberry
— with Mount Desert in the distance

the marsh on the eastern side of the island. I went the other way, skirting along the top of Gilley Beach, peering into the forests, full of odd burps and rustlings. There were sections of stone fence in the gloom, left over from the days when Little Cranberry was a populous and prosperous island, one of those self-sufficient places abounding in sheep pastures, hayfields, apple orchards, and fertile kitchen gardens.

Visitors often forget that the Maine Islands were flourishing communities long before serious efforts were made to colonize the mainland. Early settlers felt safe here; fish were plentiful (lobsters however were so abundant that indentured servants demanded contracts limiting their use to two dinners a week!); seabirds were useful for meat, bedding-feathers and plumage, and access by boat to trading communities was easy. Most of the islands today are rather sorry remnants of these once self-sustaining communities. The year-round population of Little Cranberry is less than 80.

At Maypole Point (site of the maypole and spring festival celebrations in the 18th century), strange outcrops of sharp-edged strata contrast with piles of rounded pebbles. A mile or so away, across a treacherous channel, is Deadman Point on Great Cranberry, and to the west, once again, sweeping vistas of Mount Desert Island. A narrow track leads from the beach, past a series of neat boat houses, their wooden walls silvered by sun and salt spray. Two cemeteries full of Spurlings occupy tiny patches of cleared land on the other side of the track. Then, past the broad overgrown common, we're back on Main Street.

Even after a slow beach walk there's usually plenty of time to explore the northern part of the island. One elderly gentleman, tending a garden brimming with chrysanthemums on Mosswood Road, pointed at the little paths linking the different parts of the village and providing secret routes to tranquil Bunkers Cove and the quiet north shore. I asked him about the nearby "neighborhood house," Islesford's community center.

"Bit quiet nowadays,"he told me. "Had a few dances, regular Saturday night shindigs during summer...summer folk get things livened up a bit. Most of them been coming for years just like family. Not much going on after they're gone though. Cards, gettin' gardens ready, plenty of talk but nothin' much of nothin' really. S'funny though. Time goes pretty fast. Next thing you know, they're back again." Long Maine pause. "Yup. That's 'bout it."

Well—island life isn't for everyone.

On the return journey to Northeast Harbor the sun was setting behind

Cadillac Mountain and the fir-topped islets were purple saw-tooth silhouettes against a gold and crimson sky. That's the problem with Maine on evenings like this, it looks too much like a glossy calendar. It's hard to imagine the swirling sea smoke of winter storms, the "thick-o-fogs" dense as chowder, and the clear chill of fall evenings. But, as one Downeaster put it: "If you don't like the weather here, wait a minute." He was right. When we arrived back at the dock it was raining.

Islesford — a touch of Vermont in Maine

6. Swan's Island

(Almost) A Day in a Lobster Boat

All inhabited Maine Islands have their legends, their folklore, and their cast of characters and Swan's Island is no exception. This tranquil place, home of 350 residents, delights in a history sprinkled with eccentrics and visionaries, bigger-than-life individuals who found a haven for their fantasies in this misty fiefdom.

The first settler, Thomas Kench, was a Robinson Crusoe character who arrived here in 1776, never found his Friday, and lived alone for 15 years. He was followed by the far more gregarious "King" David Smith who sired a population of 24 children from two marriages and left a lineage to which most current islanders still have claim. Then the swashbuckling Colonel James Swan, one of the original Boston Tea-party gang, purchased the island to establish a Utopia based on feudal principles, only to find himself a resident of the Paris debtor's prison for most of his life.

Today's characters, while a little less overwhelming, still give Swan's Island its idiosyncratic flavor. There was the Greek ferryman I met on the way over from Rockland, an ardent devotee of island history, island women, island wines, and mainland beer, who appointed himself my guide and lectured me at length on island ways. Thanks to him I met Fritz Johnson, "the Swede," who came as a stone cutter in 1921 and still claims the record for cutting paving blocks—786 blocks for New York streets in seven hours. He lives with his wife in a trailer below Minturn quarry, now a lovely secluded swimming hole overlooking Burnt Coat Harbor. "Still go up there on occasion and do a bit." He nodded at his two hammers, a thirty pounder and a three pounder. "Y'oughta see me do the kiss with the little one." His wife scowled, but deftly as a magician he lifted the hammer in his right hand, swung and twisted it around his head like a scimitar, missing ears and nose by millimeters, and then rested it on his lips, light as a butterfly. "Seen teeth fly with that one. Did it once with the big one for a bet. Won too!"

Swan's Island, Vinalhaven, Hurricane, Crotch, and a few others were smothered in stone cutters and carvers during the late 19th century. Rockland was their mainland mecca, a riproaring bonanza town until the decline of the 1920s. There have been a few flurries of activity since then but nothing to excite Fritz. "Quiet place now. Bit too quiet."

And so thinks Jim Bock, a relocated Larchmont lawyer, who came here full of Big Apple bombast to create a multi-layered business—restaurant, boat building yard, and lobster trap factory on the other side of Burnt Coat Harbor. Unfortunately the first years have been a little slower than expected and he fills in the day recreating authentic French harpsichords complete with hand-carved ebony and bone keys. One particular beauty, his "magnum opus," has already taken 4,000 hours and is only half complete. "I've got plenty of time. Every part of her is done with 18th century hand tools—some I made myself based on old drawings. There's no compromises with this one."

Jim has developed a close rapport with most of the island's lobstermen. They buy his wire-mesh traps and he works with them refining the details, making them strong enough for the deep waters "off island." Others are a little more wary.

Dorothy Stockbridge, who runs the Sea Breeze cafe in Mintern, thinks he may be doing too much too fast. "My land, it's not like we're against change or anything, we just usually go at things a bit more gentle. Let things grow kinda." She should tell that to her husband, Paul, who after watching me down an enormous plateful of Dorothy's famous fried clams (whole clams) offered to show me a bit of "real lobsterin" if I felt like it.

That's the kind of spontaneous invitation no traveler can resist, and so at 4:30 a.m. the following frosty morning we set out across an ice-smooth harbor in his 20 foot workboat. He brought along an assistant, a young blond-haired boy, whose first job of the morning was stuffing hand-knitted bait bags full of rotten herring.

I sat up-wind watching the first crack of crimson broaden into rosy dawn. A breeze came up with the sun and we buffeted across the waves between black islets into the Atlantic swell. Seals called to us from granite ledges and seagulls wheeled around the cabin waiting for handouts. I looked forward to a leisurely morning of hauling, sharing sandwiches and anecdotes. What I actually got was four frantic hours of hooking buoys at speed, hoisting ropes over spinning flywheels, yanking pots over the gunwale into the boat, flipping open the tops and grabbing the flailing lobsters before they grabbed us, throwing back the crabs, sea urchins, ferocious looking sculpin fish, starfish, hermit crabs, and scallops (pausing occasionally to eat them raw—a wonderful taste), refilling bait bags, clamping lids shut, hurling overboard, hauling

Old Barn - Swan's Island

Paul with his lobsters
— one of the
hardest days
of my
Journey

the next trap—an endless round of muscle-tearing tasks. In between we measured the lobsters to check legal size, wedged the claws to prevent damage, warmed numbed gloved fingers on the scalding exhaust pipe from the boat's engine, and finally, on the way back to the dock, ate bits of breakfast.

At 10:30 a.m. an exhausted city dweller staggered ashore. Paul and his boy waved and skimmed off again across the harbor for another five hours of hauling. I finished my sandwich sitting on a pile of traps waiting to recover my land legs.

And legs you certainly need on the island, either for peddling a bike up and down the hilly roads from the ferry dock at the village of Atlantic to the old lighthouse overlooking Burnt Coat Harbor, or for taking forest walks to Goose Pond from Mintern and to one of the most beautiful secluded island beaches in Maine—Fine Sand Beach.

Beyond the neat Victorian cottages in Swan's Island village, past Hancock Lodge and the simple Methodist chapel, the road curls downhill to "the carrying place", a narrow isthmus linking the eastern and western parts of the island. To the south across Toothacher Cove you can see Isle au Haut, and to the north the dramatic panorama of Mt. Desert Island. Adventurous hikers can try to reach Fine Sand Beach by trailing the pink granite ledges around Toothacher Cove. Others should follow signs through the woods along a track that becomes more and more impassable and ends in a rough turning circle at the bottom of a hill. A half-mile path laced with roots rambles through forest. Paths of emerald green sphagnum moss provide moist interludes on the journey which ends abruptly at an arc of white sand sloping to a hissing sea. Fleshy mounds of rounded pink granite enclose the beach; pines murmur and creak. If you're lucky the place will be yours a few hours, a quiet enclave of rock pools filled with whelks and periwinkles, miniature forests of Irish moss seaweed waving just below the surface of the water, broad flat rocks for sunbathing. A sense of total seclusion from the world; moments to remember.

There are tales of impending "developments" on the island, but as yet the place still retains a turn-of-the-century atmosphere. The occasional mobile home, surrounded by rusting trucks and all the paraphernalia of subsistence-living, contrasts markedly with cozy cottages and carpenter-gothic trim. People are friendly, always waving and ready to pause for a chat. There's little to do except for lobstering and the endless home improvement project which fill in the daylight hours between meals. The men gather at the general stores in

Fine Sand Beach — Swan's Island
— a magical place —

Mintern and Swan's Island to discuss traps, bait, the price of lumber, and the pettiness of "grumble-heads" (day tourists). If you ask them, they'll tell you of other secret places—small sandy coves, a tiny lily pond on the slopes of Big Mountain (elevation 218 feet!), the grave of King David near the library in Atlantic, the cliff paths around Hockamock Head lighthouse above Burnt Coat Harbor. If you're lucky enough to find accommodation you'll have time to visit them all, but if you have to make the last boat, plan a less ambitious itinerary.

I waited for the ferry by the old fog bell near the tiny library-museum. A silky evening silence settled on the open meadow where the annual lobster festival is held, and a blue heron eased itself ponderously over the spruce spikes. Islanders gathered as islanders always seem to do, just to watch the boat come in. When it arrived I expected the crazy Greek to come bounding off, but he'd been transferred to another boat; one sad young lady stood at the end of the dock alone. We both missed him.

It was a quiet ride back to Bass Harbor.

7. Vinalhaven

The Granite Island

The 15 mile, one and one-half hour trip from Rockland starts out boisterously enough as we hit open water beyond Owl's Head; a brief period of ocean-swell brings passengers to the rail, greened. Within the lee of Vinalhaven Island, the sea calms and we pass the familiar snuggling coves and smooth granite ledges topped by forests. A wooden shack peeps out from the gloom. An upturned schooner with tiny red-framed windows makes a cozy home for some seclusion-seeking summer resident, smoke eases out from a jaunty chimney. We pass Hurricane Island, a raucous shantytown of 900 granite cutters and carvers less than 60 years ago and now an Outward Bound School.

Even on a calm day the ferry moves cautiously through the narrow reach and into Carver's Harbor. Boats and lobster "cars" bob daintily near the piers, and scatterings of white houses come together in a huddle of stores and Victorian mansions along Main Street. A few islanders smile greetings and a seagull drops a little white welcome on my jacket.

Vinalhaven, one of the largest island communities on the Maine coast, is synonymous with granite. Some of the northeast's most prominent institutional structures are sheathed in the island's gray-blue bedrock. The sixty foot high columns of the Cathedral of St. John the Divine in New York came from Sand's quarry just down the road from the landing. One huge flawed block cut for the General Wool monument in Troy still lies in the grass near the fishhouses and everywhere are reminders of the island's once prime industry—piles of paving blocks, driveways of granite chips, the proud granite eagle rescued from Penn Station (ironically not an island product) near an elegant public water fountain carved and polished to a glass-like finish as a memorial to a prominent island citizen.

Up the hill from Main Street an enormous "galamander" painted bright blue stands on the village green beside the bandstand, still used for regular concerts by the island band. The galamander, with its ten foot high rear wheels, was the main form of horse-drawn transportation for moving the granite blocks from quarry to wharf. Sand's quarry alone once boasted ten of

The Galamander—Vinalhaven

these creatures along with teams of magnificently-groomed horses and a hundred yoke of oxen. Now this is the only one left and following the brief flurry of quarrying in 1970 for the new DuPont Company headquarters in Wilmington, Delaware, the industry closed down for good.

Today fishing dominates the island. Over 300 licensed lobstermen go out hauling from Carver's Harbor, Crockett and Robert's Coves, and a small fleet of seiners and draggers supply the new fish processing plant near the ferry landing. In the fall you can still see a few of the old "flakes" used for fish-drying on the west side of Carver's Harbor.

There's a lot of respect here for the "old ways." Descendants of original settler-families—Calderwoods, Coombs, Carvers, and Dyers—still comprise the majority of the 1,150 resident population. In recent years newcomers, brimming with ideas for organic gardening, solar-powered homes, community-consciousness, youth-involvement and women's liberation, have found their enthusiasm dampened by a sceptical resident population. Deliberations usually take place at Fifields on Main Street, where six or more local sages gather daily to occupy their seats near the stove. The store is true turn-of-the-century, with molded ceiling, long bowed shelves, mahogony and brass fans, and mysterious boxes smothered in dust. The fraternal gentlemen sit, still as stoics, appraising strangers and residents alike, and answering questions with the authority of supreme court justices.

Ivan Calderwood has captured all the traditional flavor of the island in his delightful series of *Uncle Dave* books reflecting "days of fellowship in Uncle Dave's fishhouse for old salts." Harold Vinal's poetry captures the mysterious beauty of these "misty, emerald-fingered islands." The residents love their books and the columned Carnegie library on the hill by the bandstand is a popular meeting place.

Further down Main Street, a breeze blows the aroma of frying clams, clam rolls, and crab patties from Tib's (open from 4 a.m. for fisherman's breakfasts), the Haven Restaurant, and the Harbor Gawker. The towers and terraces of three gracious Victorian mansions give the village the air of a spa; one of the mansions, a dowager-duchess structure with an elegant mansarded roof, has been completely cocooned in a frame of wire mesh by Bob Indiana, a resident artist, to protect its ornate trim from over-enthusiastic souvenir-hunters. His restoration plans are ambitious, but residents are disturbed by the slow pace of activity.

Guy Scarpino, a young candidate for State Representative, stands nearby offering leaflets and handshakes. " 'Bout time all this wire came down now.

A Rhythm of Roofs - Vinalhaven

Been up too long now," he complained. Guy's lively career as Israeli war veteran, kibbutz-worker, Canary Island recluse, lobsterman, and world traveler has given him a perceptive attitude to such key island problems as the decline of basic industries, high transportation costs, inflated house prices caused by "comers-in," lack of jobs for young people, alcoholism, an inadequate, poorly-maintained infrastructure and poor fishing conditions in recent years.

"Some places will just fade away," he forecasts. "Matinicus has lost its regular ferry service. Monhegan has been without proper telephones for months now. Outsiders think of island life as romantic, back-to-nature stuff, but year-rounders see it differently. There's a heck of a lot to be done."

A couple of lobstermen nod but smile sceptically. They've heard it all before. They've had their bad years when the lobsters just seem to vanish into the sub-aquatic gloom but—all in all—they wouldn't change too much. Things usually have had a way of working themselves out—at least up till now.

Day visitors will find their island time limited to about five hours and should concentrate their exploration around the town. Walking maps are available showing footpaths to the nearby Lane's Island Nature Conservancy where it is possible to wander across a broad headland of bayberry and huckleberry to the surf-sprinkled ledges. There are views of rocky inlets, little coves and a gentle arc of sand beach. In the middle of it all is the tiny Lane Cemetery with its lovely monuments and slate headstones honoring long-gone captains.

Across the bridge a footpath climbs steeply past granite quarries to the top of Armbrust Hill. Sit for a while here, looking out over Carver's Harbor and the village. Gulls rise like drifting smoke from the wharves, their cries competing with the slappy lappings of an incoming tide. Far in the distance, more than 15 miles away, you can just make out the low profile of Matinicus, one of Maine's loneliest inhabited islands. Today it is virtually inaccessible.

Then follow the wriggling path down past the new medical center and take School Street or the footpath and footbridge across Indian Creek out to the two island cemeteries near East Boston Quarry. The Robert's Cemetery has magnificent headstones, most of them carved by island artisans. One is the exact replica of a tree trunk, complete with axe marks and age rings on the branch stumps. Mr. Morton, an elderly man who tends the cemetery, admired it with me. "They used to care in those days—care about good finishing. One wrong cut and you'd smash the whole thing. They really knew their stone.''

Half a mile further east on East Main, hidden in woods, is a perfect swimming hole at Booth Quarry. On a sticky summer day there's no finer pastime than a plunge into dark cold waters enclosed by angular edges of blue-grey granite.

If there's time back in the village, visit the Historical Society museum next to the John Carver Cemetery (more superb memorials) or picnic among the woods and rocky beaches of Grime's Park at the end of West Main Street. Further up Sand's Road there are collections of fishhouses decorated with colorful garlands of buoys. Two right turns will bring you back into the bustle (a relative term) of Main Street.

Those fortunate to stay here for longer periods should explore the northern part of Vinalhaven. Near Crockett's Cove, a small worn sign points the way to Brown's Head Light. The track deteriorates and climbs steeply to a high meadow overlooking the nearby island of North Haven, a distinctly blue-blood summer colony. The small lighthouse and cottage nestle in a hollow under the bluff and in the far distance are the green and purple Camden Hills. Retracing the trail and turning south the narrow backroad leads to Tip Toe Mountain, a rugged granite pile overlooking Crockett's Cove and tiny Dogfish Island—a lovely place to watch the sunset.

As for the sunrise, try to be at Avey's Woods which surround the rocky Geary's Beach on the eastern edge of the island. You can sit in the lee of a fallen pine here and listen to the rustle of dawn, watching the cracks of color spread across the still sea. Of all my islands I found Vinalhaven the hardest to leave. I remember the people: The surly owner of Tib's cooking exquisite crab cakes at 5:30 in the morning; Andre Racz, the artist with a face like Santa Claus, beachcombing the rocky coves for bits of buoys and broken spindles for his "found object" creations; Anne and Perry Boyden who run the ARC community center and their own lives with all the open-eyed enthusiasm of children; Spencer Fuller who manages the new fish processing plant and sees a great future for the island economy, and the endless anecdotes of Ivan Calderwood, who, after six books of island tales, still has enough in his head for another six.

These Maine Islands just keep coming back.

Sneaky places.

8. Monhegan

An Island-Lover's Island

A picture to remember: four dour fishermen, worn from long days in sea-spray, giggling over a labrador puppy that keeps collapsing among lobster trap-buoys and piles of coiled rope on the dock in Port Clyde.

It was early, about 9:30 a.m. and Captain Jimmy Barstow was warming up the *Laura B.* for the daily trip out to Monhegan, 10 miles off the Maine coast. A cool breeze blew off the cove. Straggling travelers bought snacks and soda at the Port Clyde general store and wandered among rocks and pebbles below the wharves. Bags of coal, crates of milk, and boxes of eggs were being loaded onto the tiny ferry, a former army T-boat built in 1943.

At 10 a.m. promptly, the boat pulled away from the dock and passengers eased into corners among piles of cargo, watching pine-topped islets slide past as we headed for open water. On the horizon was Monhegan, "backed like a whale," waiting for us. A group of dolphins crossed the bow and turned to frolic alongside the boat. Sleepy families of gray seals filled the ledges beyond Burnt Island. Morning clouds were pulling back to reveal a bright blue day.

To many island-lovers Monhegan is the epitome of Maine islands—even of islands in general. This lonely "High Round Isle," possesses all the attributes often associated with small, self-sufficient, places—a close-knit community, high silent forests, soaring cliffs, hidden coves and beaches, and remnants of history that suggest a significance far greater than its one mile by two mile size.

Monhegan is far enough out in the Atlantic to give visitors a sense of isolation from mainland fripperies. Wandering Vikings paused here to carve grafitti on the adjunct islet of Manana, a hundred yards or so across the harbor from the mother island. When John Cabot stopped briefly in 1497, it was already a popular resting and repair center for European fishermen. Verrazano, the Italian navigator/explorer makes repeated reference to the island in his charting notes of 1524. In 1605, Captain George Weymouth harbored his vessel *Archangel* here long enough for his crew to collect supplies of fresh water, and for the captain to perform a flag and cross-raising ceremony for the benefit of the British Crown. Weymouth later made friends with the mainland

Indians, only to destroy their faith soon afterward by kidnapping five members of the tribe and hauling them off to London for public exhibition. This was the first of a long series of stupid acts by insensitive British explorers, and it's little wonder that the Maine tribes eventually tired of such treatment and joined the French (who were, apparently, far more sympathetic to the native culture) in their efforts to oust all British settlers.

Other visitors to the island during the same period included Bartholomew Gosnold, Champlain, and finally, Captain John Smith, who stayed long enough in 1614 to build seven ships and to plant a garden "on top of the rocky isle...in May that grew so well that it served for sallets (salads) in June and July." Later residents of Monhegan obviously had a high regard for Captain Smith; they erected a bronze plaque near the schoolhouse to commemorate the tercentenary of his arrival in the tight harbor.

Permanent settlement of the island began as early as 1619, and by the time the Pilgrims arrived, Monhegan's prosperity was such that the inhabitants gladly assisted the newer colonies in their efforts to establish themselves farther down the coast. Even during the early years of the French and Indian Wars in Maine, Monhegan remained a thriving bastion of trade, although by 1676 the conflict finally spread to the island and it was abandoned for almost a hundred years.

Later it revived again under the influence of a series of owner-families, the Trefethrens, Horns, and Starlings, but it never regained its former importance. The coastal ports now dominated New England trade, and Monhegan became a quiet enclave for fishermen and, much later, for a colony of artists and writers founded by Rockwell Kent. Until recently there was also a resident hermit, Ray Phillips (immortalized in Yolla Niclas' book *The Island Shepherd*), who died prior to my visit. He lived in a ramshackle hillside dwelling on Manana and rowed, once a week, across the harbor to pick up supplies from the store in Monhegan. Now his place has been taken by another young man equally devoted to the lonely life. Local sceptics are not sure how long he will endure the discomforts, particularly during the winter months.

The community of 80 permanent residents has opinions on just about every aspect of island life (some of the additional 400 summer residents—"the rusticators"—can be equally vociferous). There may not always be harmony, but tolerance is an art quickly learned here. There are the two Stanley brothers, Albert and Sherman, who appear to be the unofficial guardians of island integrity. There's the lively Dr. Alta Ashley who lives in the "Pill Box"

Monhegan

below the lighthouse, constantly curious about island life and people and alternately loved and hated for remarks in her mainland newspaper columns. There's Winnie, the retired postmistress, adored by everyone; Bill Sweetland, the young new resident, whose love of the island and the islanders is matched only by that of his closest friends, the Stanley brothers; the dignified Morton Bernstein who takes daily walks complete with walking stick down to watch the ferry arrive and walks back up the steep hill to digest the latest gossip gleaned from other islanders on the dock.

Then there are the artists, a score or more during the summer, who carry on the traditions of Rockwell Kent and his disciples. Zero Mostel had a studio here before his recent death; Jamie Wyeth visits occasionally from his own island nearby; Ruth Boynton, Reuben Tam, and Teco Slagboom find the island ideal for their work and, along with most other artists, welcome visitors to their studios during the summer.

Everyone is a "character" here. Something about the island throws its residents into high relief; quirks and idiosyncracies that might go unnoticed in a more homogeneous mainland town become the very stuff of island life here. There's little room for pretense or hypocrisy; you are simply expected to be who you are. If you're not sure who you are, islanders will help you find out, gently and genuinely. Bill Sweetland put it clearly: "You have to get on. You've got no choice."

The village itself is a tiny place, a scattering of salt-grayed shingled buildings around turn-of-the-century hostelries, a huddle of houses beneath Lighthouse Hill. At the top of the steep slope from the harbor, the track divides by one of the island stores. I took the right fork, passing Zero Mostel's old studio and the slightly lopsided 1784 House on the edge of the town pond.

A sign announces, "Caution—lobsters crossing," and a path winds through canyons of lobster traps in various stages of restoration for the winter season. Steps lead up to a fishhouse filled with old buoys, ropes, pulleys, bits of traps, browned photos of island lobstermen, and a Playboy pinup looking oddly out of place among the tackle. A table and four worn chairs by the stove complete this manly haven, a place for tall tales and beery camaraderie after blustery days in the Atlantic. The windows look down on two tiny beaches, Fish Beach and Swim Beach; across the channel the bald dome of Manana is flecked with sunshine, while Smutty Nose, a low rock ledge almost enclosing the harbor, sulks in shadow beyond the ferry dock.

The village signboard is another indication of the island's cultural climate.

Among the index cards offering the usual typing, babysitting, and house-painting services, is a petition for a Nuclear Referendum campaign, a rain-splattered map of the world showing the precise location of Monhegan, a notice for a "Beginners Workshop in Sensory Awareness," a list of artists' studios open to the public along with precise times and days, a hilarious poem in rhyming iambic pentameter honoring two departing residents, and strict instructions on island etiquette as required by the "Monhegan Associates" (no camping, no smoking, no fires, no flower picking, and so forth). The Associates are an island-protection group founded by Theodore Edison, son of the famous inventor, who own all of the land outside the village and guard it against the ravages of day-visitors.

Murdock's general store is further along on the right, a well-stocked place reflecting the refined tastes of Monhegan residents. Nearby are the Monhegan House and Trailing Yew, both charming hotels. The track continues up past the church through scrub and pines and finally emerges on a ridge overlooking the southern edge of the island. Twisted iron remnants of wrecks lie scattered across the rocks, a popular subject for photographs. During the winter lobster season, a traditionally short period from January 1st to June 25, the waters off Lobster Cove and the Washerwoman Ledges are dotted with hundreds of trap-buoys. Today the seas are clear, and rolling gently. The path narrows and sinews above Christmas Cove and Norton's Ledge. Gulls, gannets, guillemots, and an occasional puffin, circle over the gashed cliffs of Gull Rock; you can hear the surf breathing like a guru in trance and see choppy froth below Burnthead.

The path becomes even more erratic, descending into murky clefts with glimpses of swamps between the trailing yews and fallen pines, then scampering up rocks and out again on cliff tops where there are fresh breezes and views over the northern woods, and the clang of warning bells near the ledges. The island walking trail guide is deceptive. Short two-dimensional distances become tiring three dimensional struggles. Day-visitors particularly should be aware of this and avoid over-ambitious hikes.

Trails lead into Cathedral Woods from Whitehead, Squeaker Cove, and Blackhead. This is everyone's favorite place. Surf sounds are replaced by the swish of breezes in high branches. You walk on brown needle carpets through aisles of pines in a silence broken only by faint rustlings, chirpings and cooings in the shadows. Tiny flowers gleam in the ferns; roots bind exposed rocks as tautly as steel wires.

Remnants of a Wreck . Monhegan

This is a place for quiet contemplation, a place to be awed by the variety and profusion of island life. Over 600 different types of flowers have been recorded here and at least 200 species of birds.

The path passes the old ice pond and emerges on a scrub-covered ridge overlooking the village. The 1850 lighthouse is nearby on the adjoining hill, along with the island museum filled with old domestic knick-knacks and mementos of whaling days. I detoured to the cemetery, a quiet place on the hillside above the Island Inn, full of Starlings, Horns, Davises, and Trefethrens—all English names reflecting the origins of early settlers.

Down past the schoolhouse (a total of ten pupils here) the path widens to a village street again. The one-room library is on the left, dedicated to "Jackie and Edward," two young island children drowned while playing on the rocks near the harbor. It was closed but the interior brimmed with books. Tables were covered in piles of books; there were more piles in corners and the latest book of Jamie Wyeth's paintings lay open by the librarian's desk near the fireplace. Reading is obviously a popular island pastime and this small building is a hub of local culture.

Sally Murdock caught up with me as I completed my first island circuit. She and her husband, Buddy, own the general store and are often the prime catalysts of island social activities.

"You're staying at Bill's place, right?"

I'd chosen to stay at one of the island homes rather than a hotel, and Bill Sweetland's house on the cliffs overlooking the harbor was an ideal base.

"He tell you about the party for Winnie? She's the postmistress—least ways she was the postmistress. She's retiring and we're giving her a surprise party. Y'ought to come."

Sally is one of those people whose face seems in a permanent state of smile. Whatever she suggests is impossible to refuse, so I accept.

"Fine. See you later tonight at the Island Inn, in the dining room. Come in through the kitchen—they're playing fifties music mainly—it'll be fun!"

It was fun. I returned to the house and helped Bill prepare the evening meal. He brought the fish, fresh cusk, and I supplied the accompaniments—a fair arrangement which resulted in an enormous dinner washed down with two excellent bottles of California Gewürztraminer from Murdock's store.

The party began around 9 p.m. and Bill and I helped carry in the cases of beer and liquor while Bob and Mary Burton, owners of the Island Inn, supervised the proceedings. Pot luck dishes were brought by the wives and around

10 p.m. the dining room was a whirl of warm bodies reeling to Chubby Checker and Chuck Berry with occasional interludes of Mantovani for the less restless. Details of the evening elude me. I seem to remember talking to and/or dancing with each of the 60 residents who attended. Almost everyone "on-island" was here to greet Winnie and sing her praises while she sobbed happily into a pink handkerchief. The music rolled on for hours until we all finally staggered out into a brilliantly clear star-filled night and collapsed on the dewy grass, our heads struggling to adjust to clean crisp air.

I arose from bed much, much later and agreed to accompany Bill on a fishing jaunt off the eastern shore of the island. It was not a wise decision. Although amazed by the size of the cod we hauled in so easily, my body rebelled against the steady swell and we returned earlier than intended, round the northern point, past the curious seals on Seal Ledge and back into the calm harbor. While Bill cleaned and filleted the fish, I caught half a dozen arm-sized pollack just by dangling an empty hook into the clear water by the side of the boat. Handfulls of baby mussels plucked from the dock pilings made a rich sauce which we served with huge cod filets cooked in lemon, butter, and garlic. It was a long lazy evening full of stomach noises and hiccups. We exchanged tales over liqueurs and Bill gave me a condensed course in lobster-lore.

Lobsters are Monhegan's prime economy and "Trap Day" is the island's most important annual event. Way back in 1909 the lobstermen here decided to limit their season to the period from January 1st to June 25. Their reasons were highly pragmatic; first the summer season is an opportunity to make a lucrative living from tourists and short-stay residents; second, winter lobsters are renowned for their size and sweetness, whereas after June the process of "shedding" begins, which reduces both the quality and quantity of the catch. Finally, a short intense season is an excellent way to ensure conservation of a scarce resource in Monhegan's jealously guarded "territorial waters."

After Labor Day, the dozen or so lobstermen still left on the island begin the arduous process of preparing for the winter season. Boats are scraped, caulked and repainted, traps rebuilt, potheads knitted for bait, buoys painted, moorings inspected, flat rocks gathered from mainland beaches to "rock" the traps (to ensure they sink), and the customary rope lengths of 65 fathoms prepared for each trap. Most lobstermen own at least 400 traps, so the preparation is painstaking. A single error can mean the loss of a $30 trap.

During the last week in December, mountains of wire and wooden traps are moved from the paths, back yards, and front gardens down to the dock. A Grand Canyon of traps rises above the wooden pilings, each trap with its neatly coiled warp, buoy, and toggle, all waiting for the afternoon of December 31st when the boats are loaded by the lobstermen and their cadres of enthusiastic "helpers." New Year's Eve itself on Monhegan is a quiet affair, at least for the lobstermen, who are always in bed by 10 p.m. But, as dawn approaches on "Trap Day," the island explodes into life. The men scamper to their fishhouses for their "yellows," leap into skiffs to reach their boats moored in the harbor, and, with a hullaballoo of engines, move out into the swell to drop their first batch of traps in the best fishing grounds off the Atlantic coast.

They return three, four, sometimes five times during that first day to collect more traps and grab baskets of food and coffee from their wives. Trap-setting continues on into a second and third day until the island is suddenly denuded, with hardly a healthy trap to be seen anywhere. There's friendly competition, but most noticeable is the mutual care and concern of this handful of men about to undertake a six month lobstering odyssey. If one of them is taken ill and unable to set traps on Trap Day, the whole ritual is postponed until he recovers—a rare example of self-sacrifice.

Then the fun begins: the regular rounds of the traps, the rigorous hauling over the gunwales, cleaning, rebaiting, and returning of sturdy cages to the seabed, the barrels filling with green-blue lobsters, thrashing and churning. Bill has been working with Albert Stanley for a few years now but is still intrigued by the whole complex process:

"The experienced guys know every yard of the bottom for two miles out all around the island—they know instinctively where to sink the traps. I'm just starting to learn how much I don't know—on the surface it appears so simple but it takes more than a season to even begin to sense the subtleties involved. You never get bored—you get tired mind—but you're always learning. I've been out in just about every kind of weather you can imagine. That's why I like Don Stone's paintings—particularly his "Sea Smoke"—he's really caught that icy feel when the northeasters come up, the freezing vapor eating away at the sea and the boats."

"But you've got to be careful especially when it gets real cold—down to around 10 degrees. You can lose a lot of lobsters on days like that. Their bodies have a mechanism for conserving heat. If they get too cold they just shoot off their extremities—they'll drop their claws right at the knuckle where it joins the body. If you leave them in the cold air too long, when you pick

Seals — Monhegan

them up their claws'll be left lying there. You've got to get them out of the trap and into the barrel of water before they cool down too much."

"And that's only for starters—there's dozens more things you've got to look out for. One day maybe I'll be a lobsterman but it'll take a hell of a long time to know what these older guys know. Catching 15,000 pounds of lobsters apiece in six months ain't hay! Most Maine lobstermen are lucky to get 10,000 pounds in 12 months work. Monhegan's got the world's best lobsters so I reckon it's a pretty good place to be."

Monhegan is indeed a good place to be. During my brief stay I sensed fellowship and caring in the tight-knit community. There are problems, plenty of them, but the islanders seem to share an enveloping sensitivity, a larger perspective on life, a recognition of the fleeting nature of personal difficulties and mishaps.

On my last day I stood on the deck of the *Laura B.* watching them meet as they do each day on the dock, to talk of island things—to see and be seen. For a brief moment I wanted to be one of them, to share their commitment and their mutual dependence. Rockwell Kent, in prose as delicate as his paintings, felt the same way:

> *Truly, I loved that little world—that small sea-girt island, a seeming floating speck in the infinitude of sea and sky; one was as though driven to seek refuge from the cosmic intensity in a closer relationship to people and to every living thing.*

But the boat moved away and I went with it.

9. Cliff Island

A Quiet Corner of Casco Bay

A scene out of Dickens: night-black along cobbled streets edged by brick warehouses and tiny stores with multi-pane windows, handcarved wooden tavern signs catching the glimmer from Victorian street lamps, the tang of ocean drifting up cat-quiet alleys.

This is Portland—the old restored portside area of Portland, Maine. The streets were slippery with a combination of dew and fine sea haze and I seemed to be the only one about at 4:45 a.m. on a chilly October morning.

I walked past the old Port Tavern where I'd spent the previous evening sea-shantying with a bunch of sailors on a three day binge before returning to the mundane disciplines of ocean life. We finally rolled out into the night after a particularly rousing chorus of "Liverpool Nell" and vowed undying devotion to one another and to the spirit of free adventure.

This morning, however, I felt neither free nor adventurous. The hollow clang of my boots on the cobbles sounded like an orchestra of gongs inside my head. At the bottom of the hill slivers of mist wafted between lamp posts like lost wraiths doomed to an eternity of aimless drifting. Ahead of me I could hear the waters of Casco Bay slopping against the pilings and bulkheads of the harbor.

The idea of exploring the bay with a head pounding like a jackhammer on a day that promised nothing but drizzle and damp mists, appeared a little ludicrous. Also the idea of picking one tiny island out of a slightly exaggerated total of 365 islands and islets ("one for every day of the year" as they say locally) seemed ridiculous. Only memories of the barman's enthusiasm gave me the wherewithal to continue through the gloom.

"Cliff Island—that's the spot. They're all lovely places, mind—the Diamonds, the Chebeaques, Peak's, Long Island, Bailey—but Cliff's special. There's not so many people around, maybe 100 tops in winter—it's a pretty quiet place. Good place for walking. A lot of the others have gone suburban—people commuting into Portland every day—but Cliff's different, keeps itself to itself a bit more."

Thanks to barman Edward, long-time lover of the bay and avid weekend fisherman, I found myself groping along Custom House wharf looking for signs for the Casco Bay ferry. It was dark as a cave except for the glimmer of a dockside snack bar. The inside was all worn green and cream under fluorescent strips. Steam curled up to a high smoke-stained ceiling from two large urns. A line of sleepy-faced men sat by the counter eyed by jelly-filled doughnuts piled in a sticky pyramid on a plate under a glass cover. There were signs implying a wealth of early morning breakfast snacks but everyone seemed to have a doughnut with a red eye, uneaten, in front of them.

Coversation consisted of a muffled rumble of grunts and half-hearted expletives. The young girl behind the counter was reading a paper-back romance with a pastel cover showing a well-endowed lady in the throes of ecstacy, watched over by two square-jawed gentleman— a Tom Selleck-type with a moustache and a Tom-Selleck type without a moustache. The waitress's bosom heaved. She seemed put out by my interruption and poured me a sloppy cup of coffee, bitter and lukewarm. I had no desire for a red-eyed doughnut but she looked at me in amazement when I asked for an alternative.

"That's all we've got—just those." She nodded her head toward the sticky pile. I declined and she resumed her reading.

At 5 a.m. I boarded the ferry outside the snack bar. It still felt a little crazy getting up so early for a boat but the next trip was not until 10 a.m. and I wanted as much time as possible to explore Cliff Island before the last return boat at 6:45 p.m.

I was one of five chilly passengers and we all sat huddled in different corners of the upper deck as the *Abenaki* eased down the narrow dock into the harbor, hooting at the darkness. The mists had now coalesced into a fog and our searchlights reflected back at us.

Somehow this eerie limbo seemed appropriate for a bay full of mysteries. Tales of ghosts, and buried treasures, and strange Indian legends abound here. Almost every island in this 200 square mile tangle of islands has its story. Orr's Island, for example, is where the unfortunate Mr. and Mrs. Wilson met their grisly ends. Mr. Wilson, a local fisherman-farmer went hunting one Thanksgiving on the island. After he failed to return by evening his wife set out searching for him. According to the legend, they both vanished. Friends organized a rescue party the following day and rowed to the island only to find two human skeletons sitting upright against a rock surrounded by the skeletons of twelve wolves, all picked clean. No one knows what happened or what kind of creature could devour so much flesh in so little time.

Some of the tales have a real fisherman's-yarn quality to them. Michael Mitton for example, one time owner of Peak's Island, claimed to have been attacked by a triton or merman who attempted to drag him and his boat into the depths. The quickwitted Mitton promptly picked up an axe and severed both hands of the creature who vanished into the depths of the bay. According to Mitton the hands continued to cling to the side of the boat until he pried them loose and flung them away, unfortunately before anyone could verify his claims.

Then there is the haunted cellar on Great Chebeaque island. This notorious spot is protected by ghost horses whose thundering hooves can be heard whenever anyone seeks the pirate's treasure said to be hidden here at Rose's Point. A new house built over the cellar subsequently became one of the most wraith-plagued places in the whole bay, constantly reverberating to the cries of horses and deep groans from the depths. The banging of clubs against the outside walls of the house and the terrifying "guardian of the cellar," a horribly bleeding aparition, which greeted the curious as they opened the door to the cellar steps, completed the spectacular show.

Perhaps the best-known tale is that of Captain Keiff, Cliff Island's own miserable villain, who made a living by setting up false beacons along the island shore and misleading ships onto the razor-edged ledges of the eastern bluffs. As the vessels were pounded by the waves, he would murder the survivors, bury them in a flat meadow back from the bluffs now known as "Keiff's Garden," and salvage the cargoes for his own profit. On stormy nights, so islanders say, you can still hear the screams and groans from the corpses in the meadow.

After a couple of brief stops at Long Island and Great Chebeaque, we slowly nudged against the wharf at Cliff Island. The fog was lifting and a gray dawn light eased over the silhouetted pines. A group of noisy school children scrambled aboard and all was chaos for a few minutes. Then the ferry gave a toot and vanished into the mists leaving me alone and damp at 6:30 a.m. with nowhere to breakfast and no clear plans for the rest of the day.

Ah, the joys of island exploration!

Immediately ahead of me lay the island nexus, a crossroads of sorts with a small green and a flagpole erected in 1981 to the memory of a Mr. Berle. Nearby was a tennis court with a stern notice attached to the wire mesh requesting parents to keep a tight rein on errant children who disturbed the peace of the island and misused the court. A notice board had little index cards pinned to it offering lawn mowing services, wood chopping, house cleaning, laundry at

Casco Bay Boats

60¢ a pound, and a pram for sale. A rather sad note read: "Lost—a white envelope with cash belonging to the Cliff Island School Children."

The smell of burning wood wafted past the island hall and library next to the tennis court and somewhere away in the distance someone was chopping wood.

The houses were neat, trim Victorians sitting on neat, trim lawns. Curtains were still drawn in the bedrooms and smoke was just beginning to curl out of chimneys. A dog barked and was answered by another in the mist. Two red-winged blackbirds pecked for worms on the green.

Cliff is a high rocky spine of land about two miles long and less than a mile wide at the broadest point. A parallel but shorter sliver known as The Bluff lies half a mile east of the main island linked by sand flats, salt marshes, and beaches. It takes about two minutes to walk across from the ferry landing on the west side to the cozy cove littered with lobster traps on the east side. An enormous 1968 Cadillac Coupe de Ville, ingeniously converted into a trailer, sprawled in the grass overlooking boats in a natural rocky barbor.

A short distance down the road the Seventh Day Adventist church, the only church on the island, and the schoolhouse, sat side by side. The school was a simple clapboard affair full of books, nooks, charts, maps, paintings, plants, and class projects—stimulating even to this jaded student. The church, on the other hand, seemed rather aloof and empty, five wooden pews, an enormous stove, and lots of cold gray space. Across the road a sign in the McVane house window read "Please be careful when coming in—the bird may be flying around."

At Bob and Anita Buttrick's store overlooking Fishermen's Cove there were signs of life. It turned out to be an early morning lobsterman filling his trap-laden work boat with gasoline. "We use the honor system here. Fill her up and write it in Bob's little book. Works just fine." The lobsterman smiled and his face buckled like a crunched beer can. "You look like y'could use some coffee." At last—restoration. "And a bit of s'thing to make it go down smooth." He poured me a cup from a thermos flask and added a generous splash of bourbon from a Jim Beam bottle. "Gets you going right—right?"

I nodded enthusiastically, gulped the fiery concoction and, as if by divine arrangement, three shafts of early morning sunlight thrust through the haze and set the water bouncing with old gold. The dozen or so boats moored in the cove rocked together in a light swell as the lobsterman prepared to leave on his early morning rounds of trap-pulling.

"Store won't be open for quite a while now. You okay for food?" Stupidly, I'd forgotten my usual emergency supplies. Without waiting for a response he reached into his pocket and flung me a couple of chocolate bars. "Should keep you going awhile. Enjoy yourself." And with a growling engine and a lot of blue smoke, my Good Samaritan eased away from the landing and disappeared into the mists.

It was silent again. Dew dripped off leaves into small morning puddles and another of the island's red wing blackbirds pecked among the road stones near my feet. I felt the whole place belonged to me and a happy bourbon-buzz crept down my spine and warmed my toes.

The track eased downhill to the sandy flats between the main island and The Bluff. Marsh grass and bullrushes filled the low land; seagulls promenaded together across the mud-colored sands of a small beach overlooking Fishermen's Cove. The track curved gently through the high grasses and led to a broader beach on the north side of the promontory, a perfect place to spend a summer afternoon. The morning was still chilly, however, so I kept walking and climbed up the side of The Bluff to a ridge topped by windshaped pines. A large house full of windows occupied an area of cleared land to my left. It looked very empty, closed up for the winter, a few bits of barbecue equipment rusting forlornly on the terrace.

From the top of The Bluff I could look down 100 feet or more at a churning ocean, pushing foamy fingers into the sharp strata. The rock surface was black and etched like wood grain; bright veins of quartz squirmed across the serrations, occasionally broadening into globular "eyes," and soft patches of mica broke off in my hands separating into transparent wafers.

To the east I could just make out the hazy shape of Jewell Island, one of Casco Bay's secluded delights. This 220 acre patch of rock, pines, and tiny beaches, is named after George Jewell who purchased the island from local Indians in 1637 for "a horn of powder, a bottle of rum, and half a dozen fish hooks." All remained tranquil until the Indian Wars when a number of settlers were killed here in a vicious massacre. Then, a century or so later, tales of buried pirate treasure brought scores of ragtaggle prospectors, "gold-diviners," soothsayers, and "second-sighters," who picked and poked among the coves in search of an elusive wooden chest reputedly left by the notorious Captain Kidd under "a great flat rock of enormous weight." The rocky beach of Punch Bowl at the southern end was a popular digging ground although the whole island seems to have been worked over at one time or another.

Today, fortunately, the search seems to have been abandoned and the island smiles to itself peacefully on the fringe of the bay, disturbed only rarely by visitors.

Somehow I lost the cliff-edge path along the top of The Bluff and found myself floundering around in a dense scrub of sumac, juniper, bayberry, and poison ivy. Stubbornly I continued, trying to find safe footholds on the increasingly knife-like surface of the linear rock—almost a microcosm of the thin rocky islands that fill Casco Bay. After a while I realized that going back would offer as many problems as pressing forward through the tangle. It was very lonely—just the rock, the waves, and the dark line of pines along the ridge. I began to wonder what would happen if I broke an ankle in this desolate place. There was no path; it appeared no one ever came this way. The mists only increased my sense of isolation.

Somehow—I'm not quite sure how—I managed to struggle over the ridge and down to the tidal flats of the western lee shore, only to find pools of gray mud and rocks smothered in slick green algae. By the time I finally scrambled onto firm hard sand among piles of driftwood and bits of wrecked boats, I was a bleeding, bruised, mud-stained mess of sweating flesh and beginning to lose patience with myself and Cliff Island in general.

I followed part of a nature trail set up by local school children which led to a sports field. Green grass, and—at last—sunshine.

"Bin on't Bluff?" An elderly gentleman was walking his terrier across the meadow and seemed amused by my appearance. "Lucky y'didn't get hurt. It's bad on that place."

I tried a smile but it remained a scowl.

Back on the island's main road that loops around the central rocky spine, the morning turned golden and warm. The mud dried, the bramble scratches stopped stinging, and I ate one of the lobsterman's chocolate bars while following a gravel track through a forest of silver birch and high pines. A spur turned off to the northern tip of the island, past summer cottages, all shuttered. It narrowed to a path meandering through a ferny wood with views out across the bay from modest cliffs. The air was very still. I could hear fishermen discussing family affairs and island business on their CB boat radios. Monarch butterflies flitted through pine branches and the last curlicues of mist.

The woods ended and I stood on a ledge overlooking the northern tip of the island, a broken promontory of bayberry and juniper scattered over outcrops of bedrock. Ahead was a panoramic vista of calm ocean and pine-covered

Rock Strata - The Bluff
— a wonderful
mini-landscape of
whorls and
knife edge ridges
— always moving

islets under a blue mackerel sky. Great Chebeaque lay off to my left and skinny Bangs Island immediately ahead. Bailey Island and Merriconeag Sound were blocked from view by a scattering of ledges, some too small to be named.

There's nothing to do here really but sit and enjoy the view, and that's what I did, watching tiny white workboats skittering across the water and gulls dive-bombing the discards of lobster pots as they were emptied and thrown back by aproned fishermen.

The sun was warm and I dozed a little, awakening sharply to see a middle-aged man peering down at me—a tanned, smiling face topped by curly black hair. He was dressed in white T shirt, jogging shorts, and sneakers, and looked very pleased with himself and the world in general.

"Hi, I'm Paul McVane."

My mentor had arrived. It's always a good idea on islands to spend time with the residents and see the community through their eyes—the visit becomes more meaningful. Their snippets of island history and tradition provide depth to everything you see. Paul was the perfect host, a relaxed individual with a passion for the local Seventh Day Adventist Church (the few remaining members still celebrate the Sabbath on Saturdays), and for mowing lawns. At one time he claimed to have taken care of 75 different lawns on Cliff. As there are 60 summer cottages and 40 "year round" homes, he had a virtual lawn-care monopoly on the island.

We strolled back through the woods to his home near the ferry landing. He told anecdotes about island residents and we passed the house of Miss Johanna Von Tiling, a retired school teacher, well-known singer of lieder, and one of Cliff's prominent citizens. "Lovely person," murmured Paul. "Full of life. She never seems to stop—she's helped keep this place alive."

There was a period a few years ago when Paul thought the island might "die" as a community. It has happened elsewhere in Maine although usually to more inaccessible places. There was talk of closing the local junior school, which had only six pupils. The resident population was decreasing, lobstering was not the lucrative livelihood it had once been, the high school children were already being ferried daily to school in Portland, and there was some doubt as to whether the store could stay open. Trade was down and the costs of importing all supplies were increasing.

"It was a real bad time," Paul told me. "We decided we had to give it our best shot. The first thing was to increase the number of children at the school to eight—that's the required minimum. So we all got together, winterized a vacant house, neighbors chipped in with time and materials, and then we invited a family over—it was a poor family, on welfare in the city at the time. They had three children and they loved the idea. So—that saved the school. And in the last few years the situation's got a little better. I think Cliff'll make it now."

Paul handed me a pile of local community newsletters. *The Cliff Island Sea Gull,* a lively quarterly brimming with poetry by residents, essays, general news, and island gossip. If this little paper is anything to go by, Cliff is a constant whirl of school bakes, library luncheons, charity dances, auctions, poetry readings, and kid's parties. The most active time is during July and August when island olympics are held on the playing fields near The Bluff. Usually in late August there's an Old Timer's Day.

"Almost like the old days—the real old days," Paul told me. "There used to be boarding houses here and a hotel—the Aucocisco House—Mrs. Batchel's place. Full up every summer until the Germans started running U-boats up and down the coast, 'specially around Boston, and it scared everybody off. They were frightened the ferry would be sunk. So the place went bankrupt and later there were tales of ghosts and odd goings on. They finally had to pull it down, things got so bad."

I asked Paul about the winters on the island.

"Oh we've all got snow shoes. Some go cross-country skiing and the lobstermen's families spend a lot of time mendin' gear, knitting heads, going over pot warp, replacing trap-laths, and painting up the buoys. Time soon goes. It's spring before you know."

I left Paul's house stuffed with stories—tales of Indian shell mounds in hard-to-find places, of cannonballs occasionally unearthed on the island, including a 25 pound beauty found by Paul, and anecdotes about the abundant wildlife here, deer, mink and racoon, not to mention a few odd people who live deep in the forest and keep very much to themselves.

Totally by chance I found one such "hermit's" house on a stroll I took toward the southern tip of the island. This portion of Cliff is less developed and houses are hidden down tracks, deep in the dark woods. Unfortunately I never met the owner but was told he was a young man, a Vietnam vet and rather quiet, "in a friendly kind of way."

His house is one of those places hopeful hermits dream about—a tiny self-built A-frame sheltered in pines with windows overlooking the bay, and a natural boat ramp. His yard was neatly organized: three piles of cleanly chopped wood of different sizes all covered with tarpaulin, stacks of lobster traps surrounded by coiled ropes, buoys, and large plastic barrels for the catch, an

Johanna Von Tiling
—Cliff Island
dynamo—

outside refrigerator stocked with cold beer and basics, a small outbuilding used as a toilet; everywhere a sense of perfect harmony and order.

Inside was similar, a single room equipped with all the necessities of the simple life—gas oven, wood-burning stove, stereo and TV, CB radio, sofa covered in a quilt, scattered rugs, well-stocked library with a bias towards ecology, carpentry, and small-scale farming. On the low table was a manual for constructing a solar greenhouse, and, in the corner by the stereo, a delicate model of the house itself, obviously a feature of pride.

Above the kitchen was a raised platform reached by a rough-cut ladder which housed the bed and more piles of books. Sunlight trickled through segments of stained glass. And that, basically, was it. A totally self-sufficient home—economical, cozy, and full of its owner's personality. I wish I'd met him.

But I did meet Miss Tiling, school teacher, opera singer, and island dynamo. I was waiting by the landing for the evening ferry to Portland when a striking elderly lady in a thick fur coat and glasses walked purposefully down the main street. She had a bun of silver-white hair hidden under a brown bonnet and a silk scarf around her neck.

"I know who you are," she informed me in an authoritative voice. "Paul told me you spent the afternoon with him submerged in our little newspapers." I nodded, shook hands, and for the next hour we never stopped talking.

She told me of her early visits to the island in the 1920s when her father, a physician, bought a summer cottage here. After her mother's death she and her father moved permanently to the island. She has lived here since 1949 with occasional mainland sorties, often in support of island interests, and, more rarely now, to give concerts of her beloved German songs.

"The winters were a little difficult at first," she told me as we stood together on the ferry watching the island move away into the haze. "We had only one electric socket, there was no insulation—it was a summer cottage, you see—so to keep warm we had to bring in cartload after cartload of coal and wood. But I kept thinking, if I can make it through the first one I'll manage all the rest. And I did, and I'm still here."

And that's the spirit that makes these islands such memorable places to visit and to live in.

I'll be going back to Cliff.

10. The Isles of Shoals

A Poet's Haven

As islands go the Shoals are tiny, very tiny—a straggle of bare rocky islets ten miles out in the Atlantic from Kittery, Maine, smoothed into rotund docility by glaciers, tides, and gales. Officially there are nine of them: Appledore, Smuttynose, Malaga, Cedar, and Duck are on the Maine side of the border; Star, White, Seavey's, and Londoner's are in New Hampshire.

These fragments have attracted more than their fair share of interest and activity ever since Captain John Smith commended them as "the remarkablest Isles for Landmarks" and bestowed his name, "the Smyths Isles," on the archipelago. His description of them as: "Many barren rocks, the most overgrowne with such shrubs and sharpe whins you can hardly passe through them; without either grasse or wood, but three or foure shrubby old Cedars", hardly seems to reflect an enthusiastic attitude, yet enthusiastic he was to the point of claiming: "And of all foure parts of the world that I have yet seene not inhabited, I would rather live here than anywhere..."

His plans to establish a colony never materialized, but others after him managed to create a series of viable settlements which, by the mid-seventeenth century, boasted a substantial population of around 650. They were mostly fishermen famous for their "dun-fish," a special kind of dried cod considered far superior to the Newfoundland variety. From all accounts these were worthy, god-fearing people who lived by strict rules of conduct which excluded all women from the island until 1648, when a resolute young man named Reynolds challenged the local powers by bringing his wife and fighting his case all the way up to the General Court of Massachusetts. In a rather half-hearted verdict the court ruled that "if no further complaint come against her she may enjoy the company of her husband."

The affluent complacency of these tiny communities was shattered by the Revolution. Most Shoalers scattered to the mainland towns, leaving behind a raggle-taggle bunch of loose-living individuals whose antics during the early 1800s caused the church to send out emergency teams of fire-and-brimstone ministers, determined to salvage souls wherever possible. They had a hard time of it. One writer recorded the scene in tremulous Victorian prose:

A state of apathetic indolence has falled upon the islanders who appear to have forgotten the world, and whom the world seems to have forgotten, until the condition of poverty and deprivation into which those who remained had lapsed became a matter of public scandal.... In some drunken orgie the shoalsmen had burned their meeting house to the ground. Then for want of a guiding hand, the always loosely-bound society had fallen into the worst depths of immorality. Men and women were found living together, with children born to them outside of wedlock. A new generation was growing up like the weeds among the rocks, who perhaps had never heard the name of God spoken except to blastpheme with, or known any difference between one day of the week and another.... That such things could happen in a Christian land is indeed hard to believe; but it is all true.

Outrage turned to action. Preaching was resumed, a new school was founded, the unmarried were married, and the church rebuilt in Gosport on Star Island. Then, setting the seal on an altogether brighter future, Thomas Laighton of Portsmouth (despairing of New Hampshire political shenanigans) came with his wife and children in 1839, to live a hermit's life as the White Island lighthouse keeper.

After a few years he moved to Smuttynose Island, also totally deserted, and assisted by his family, began to take in summer visitors. His wife's cooking, particularly her fish chowders, broiled mackerel, and apple pandowdy, and the charm of this self-sufficient family, attracted the attention of mainland notables. Trade increased and in 1848 Thomas opened his Appledore House on Appledore Island, thus becoming a serious inn-keeper and owner of one of the nation's first summer resorts.

Artists, writers, composers, and philosophers flocked to his isolated retreat to enjoy the food, their own mutual company, and Thomas' delightful daughter, Celia, who read her little snippets of poetry and prose to such as Hawthorne, Whittier, Richard Henry Dana, and James Russell Lowell.

Somehow these ragged little humps of white rock and sawgrass brought out the romantic spirit in famous literati. Hawthorne gushed rapturously in his *American Note Books:*

The Lighthouse on White Island

It is quite impossible to give an idea of these rocky shores—how confusedly they are bound together, lying in all directions: what solid ledges, what great fragments thrown out from the rest...as if some of the massive materials of the world remained superfluous after the Creator had finished, and were carelessly thrown down here, where the millionth part of them emerged from the sea, and in the course of thousands of years have become partially bestrewn with a little soil.... Pour the blue sea around these islets, and let the surf whiten and steal up from their points, the northwest wind the while raising thousands of whitecaps, and the evening sun shining solemnly over the expanse—and it is a stern and lovely scene.

Lowell, in his *Pictures from Appledore*, lapses into sonorous verse:

Look southward for White Island light;
The lantern stands ninety feet o'er the tide.
There is first a half-mile of tumult and fight,
Of dash and roar and tumble and fright,
And surging bewilderment wild and wide,
Where the breakers struggle left and right.
Then a mile or more of rushing sea,
And then the lighthouse slim and lone.

Even the demure Mrs. Partington, a well known poetess of the day, struggled between her sense of the ridiculous and her feeling for the sublime as she parodied Byron's famous ode:

The Isles of Shoals! the Isles of Shoals!
Where tuneful Celia loved and sung,
Where the free billow ever rolls,
Where Oscar rose and Cedric sprung;
The summer glory gilds their shore,
And crowns the cliff of Appledore.

Celia doubtless blushed at such compliments and continued to pen her poetry, much to the admiration of her summer visitors who vied with one another to attend her evening soirees in a flower-filled parlor overlooking the ocean, and listen to her limpid lines:

> *...to feel the wind sea-scented on my cheek*
> *To catch the sound of dusky flapping sail....*

Her fame spread as her works were published in *Atlantic Magazine. Land-Locked,* was the first in 1861, and her editor, James T. Field, encouraged her to write prose pieces on the history and strange charms of these rocky fragments, to tell the tales of early settlers, island ghosts, visits by Blackbeard (the "Pirate of the Shoals"), the wreck of a Spanish galleon, and the grisly death of its crew, and to describe the simple joys of isolated island life.

Celia was delighted: "Ever have I longed to speak these things that make life so sweet; to speak the wind, the clouds the bird's flight, the sea's murmur." The result was *Among the Shoals,* published in 1873, one of her best works and lauded by Van Wyck Brooks as "a hooked rug in prose, woven of pure materials, in harmonious colors."

The Shoals became a fashionable summer retreat. A new hotel, *The Oceanic,* opened on Star Island in 1873 and everything looked rather rosy until a terrible murder the same year on lonely Smuttynose Island. There are various versions of the tale but little doubt exists about the guilt of Louis Wagner, a fisherman, who rowed over to the island from Portsmouth one evening in March and cold-bloodedly butchered Karen Christensen and her sister-in-law, Anethe, before ransacking the house in search of money and valuables. Karen's sister, Maren, somehow escaped with her dog, and hid behind a large boulder at the far eastern edge of the island, half a mile from the house. After hours of lonely terror in the snow, she managed to attract the attention of men working on the new hotel and the pursuit of Wagner began.

He was finally caught and sentenced to execution. Appeals, a brief escape, and public debate on the ethics of capital punishment, delayed his death until June 25, 1875, well over two years after the murders. To the end Wagner claimed his innocence and accused Maren and her husband John of killing the women and pocketing their savings. Local newspapers did in fact confirm that after the hanging, Maren went insane and confessed to the crime, but the public generally ignored such afterthoughts and Wagner remains very much the culprit to this day.

The Turnstile
on Star Island

For a while the notoriety of tiny Smuttynose attracted the curious and ghoulish, but gradually the popularity of Star and Appledore island summer resorts waned as mainland competition grew. By the early 1900s the hotels were closed and in 1914 Appledore House was destroyed by fire. It was only the later adoption of Appledore by the University of New Hampshire as a center for marine biology that saved some of the remaining buildings from oblivion. Where Julius Eichberg once played Beethoven sonatas and Celia read her tender poems, now young ornithologists come for summer courses and study the mating habits of the black-backed and herring gulls in the quiet coves.

Star Island also has its devotees. In addition to the participants at religious conferences organized by the Unitarians and Congregationalists in a series of new and restored buildings (including the imposing *Oceanic Hotel* itself), hundreds of day visitors arrive on the *Viking Queen* ferry from Portsmouth (N.H.) for a three hour guided tour and exploration of the island. The restoration attempts to capture the character of Gosport, the seventeenth century fishing village removed to make way for *The Oceanic Hotel*. The cottages are a mixture of white clapboard and stone; the old turnstile has been rebuilt and neatly frames Gosport church, perched on the island's highest knoll. To the south the lovely lighthouse on White Island still flashes over the reefs and ledges and the enclosed walkway linking it to the lightkeeper's cottage. To the north you can clearly see the remnants of the Appledore House cottages and outbuildings, some restored and others slowly crumbling into the bayberry bushes.

Even with their summer visitors, these lonely outposts off the coast of Maine and New Hampshire retain their quiet charm and calm. Wander the reefs and coves; take a book of Celia Thaxter's work and read the descriptions of her beloved islands. This is sunset:

> *The whole heaven was in a blaze of scarlet, across which sprang a rainbow unbroken by the topmost clouds, with its seven perfect colors chorded in a triumph against the flaming background; the sea answered the sky's rich blue, and the gray rocks lay drowned in melancholy purple. I hid my face from the glory—it was too much to bear.*

Islands seem to bring out the poet in everyone.

11. Cuttyhunk

A Tiny Patch of Sand and Sumac

The scarlet and cream ferry boat, the *Alert*, gave a few burps of smoke and moved slowly across the harbor, past rusting trawlers and huddles of Portuguese fishermen.

Herman Melville's old whaling town of New Bedford, once the fourth largest port in the United States, has always been a place of refuge, originally for stern-principled Quakers, then for slaves escaping from the south along the "Underground Railroad," and more recently for many Portuguese families. Today it enjoys a pleasantly contented pace of life, and is seemingly reluctant to encourage the steel and concrete transformation of cities closer to New York. The old cobbled streets down by the waterfront have been relaid, a glass-making factory re-opened on North Second Street, complete with museum, Melville's pew has been carefully preserved in the Seamen's Bethel on Johnny Cake Hill opposite the Whaling Museum, and dozens of ship chandlers and marine-related businesses are clustered near the wharves, serving the fishing fleet which has been a feature of the city since the mid-eighteenth century. The Rodman Candleworks is now an attractive restaurant, as is the Bourne Counting House across the road on Steamship Pier next to Louie's, a famous seafood eatery loved by the tourists who throng to the Martha's Vineyard ferry during the summer months. While up to 450 passengers sit sardined in plastic seats on the decks of *M/V Schamonchi*, a few hardy travelers find space where they can on the Cuttyhunk island ferry, among boxes of groceries, piles of cedar shingles, reinforcing rods, and suitcases.

The day is bright and calm. We pass another aging Portuguese trawler and the melancholy sounds of a traditional "fado" song trickle out from a rusty porthole. Across the harbor the towered and spired skyline of Fairhaven sparkles in the morning sun. New Bedford itself has a more ponderous profile of domes and Doric-columned buildings, a place of banks and hardy institutions, once the richest city in America, and according to ardent devotee, Melville, "the dearest place to live in, in all New England."

"Second dearest, more like. Cuttyhunk first, New Bedford next." Oliver Stevens and his wife sit on the narrow bench by the wheelhouse, smiling at the blue silhouette on the horizon. Their links with the island go back three generations and they have finally decided to live on Cuttyhunk permanently once they complete the insulation of Mrs. Steven's great grandfather's cottage. "We're at the intriguing stage now," says Oliver. "Everywhere we lift the old floorboards we find piles of New Bedford and New London newspapers, all dated in the 1880s. A real collection and still readable!"

The science-fiction writer, Hilbert Schenck, discusses the latest world crises with the crew, and every so often sneaks a peep at the island emerging from the morning haze.

There are only six passengers on the *Alert*. "It's off season now, much better time to visit," Oliver tells me. "Summer's not that bad, mind, although at the peak they bring two lots a day and that can get a little hectic for a few hours. Old Norm flies in too—Norman Gingrass—he brings his seaplane over from Fairhaven. Now that's a lovely way to arrive and you get a much longer spell on the island."

This tiny speck of land barely two miles long and less than a mile wide, could have become one of New England's most historic sites, for it was here that Bartholomew Gosnold and his thirty-two-man crew landed on May 25, 1602, intending to start a colony, possibly for Sir Walter Raleigh. The stone tower at the western end of the island, built in 1903, marks the site of the first English habitation on the coast of New England. According to Gosnold's records, there were exuberant celebrations that led inevitably to over-indulgence: "The powder of sassafras in twelve hours cured one of our company that had taken a great surfeit by eating the bellies of dogfish, a very delicious meat."

It was this sassafras, covering the island, that sealed the fate of the little colony. It appears that Gosnold was not particularly trusted by his crew, for when he proposed to return to England with a valuable cargo of sassafras, leaving behind most of his men, there was almost instant rebellion. Gosnold assured them he intended to make a lucrative sale, buy fresh supplies, and return early the following year to the island. He almost persuaded them, and many of the crew began to lay out a plantation as Gosnold went off to explore another island in the Elizabeth chain. But unfortunately he didn't return when expected, and food supplies on Cuttyhunk ran out. One of the sailors, Gabriel Archer, wrote in his diary that the men were "in a dumpish terror"

Cuttyhunk — a place of quiet spaces

and were obliged to live on "alexander and sorrel pottage, ground nuts and tobacco." To make matters worse, a member of the crew was wounded by Indians who were angered that Gosnold had stolen one of their canoes. When Gosnold finally came back a few days later, the crew had rejected all ideas of plantations and colonies. They chose instead to sail home to ensure they received their share of the sassafras profits and the island was abandoned.

During the great whaling years of the nineteenth century Cuttyhunk became the headquarters for many of the navigational pilots who guided the ships through the narrows between the islands and into New Bedford. In 1864 the exclusive Cuttyhunk Club was founded as a center for the rich man's sport of bass fishing, and in 1921, William Wood, owner of the vast American Woolen company, took over the club's interests and even attempted to buy up the whole island for use as a private resort. His attempt failed, but he went ahead and constructed the huge stone mansion that still towers above the village. Just below the mansion is another Wood creation, the rambling Avalon Club, owned until recently by Frank Sinatra's theatrical agent.

We could see the two monoliths clearly as we entered Cuttyhunk Pond, a placid cove surrounded by low hills and sand bars. The small gray and white cottages of Gosnold Village littered the slopes of Lookout Hill, below a huge experimental wind-powered generator shaped like an aircraft propellor and similar to those installed on nearby Block Island.

"It's a good idea," said Oliver. "Trouble is it's too efficient for its own good. During one storm just a couple of months ago they couldn't stop it—they tried the brakes and everything—but it just kept whirling away until the wind dropped. People here got nervous. They weren't too keen on the idea of those three blades flying off in a gale and decapitating a few roofs. So it's locked up now for a while at least until someone decides what to do next."

Cuttyhunk feels like one of those lonely Orkney islands off the west coast of Scotland, denuded of trees, a primitive wind-smoothed profile with a thin covering of summer-bleached grasses and bayberry.

Another resident joined us as we chugged across the pond to the dock and pointed at a particularly bleak hill tied to the main island by a tenuous strip of sand. "That's Copicut Neck. It was a leper colony once. If you live out there you're really pioneering. You've got to get your own water and your own power. They're not linked up yet."

A few lonely houses peered out forlornly across the bayberry clumps. Four black cormorants skimmed across the water, their shadows bouncing on ripples. To the south the tall cliffs of Gay Head on Martha's Vineyard rose up from a gunmetal-blue ocean.

"And that's No Man's Land out there, off the cliffs." The resident seemed to enjoy painting dismal word pictures. "Taboo territory that. Naval flyers keep using it for target practice and no one's allowed on." He pointed south now. "Those are the other islands in the Elizabeth chain. The big one there is Nashawena where the Forbes family live. That's taboo too plus there's a ghost." He looked deadly serious and I was glad to be off the boat and walking with Hilbert Schenck briskly up to Gosnold village.

"We're an idiosyncratic lot," Hilbert commented and pointed to a crudely painted piece of grafitti on the road surface which read: "REDRUM," in blood-red paint. "We're a well-read lot too—even the grafitti's got literary pretensions. You remember Stephen King's book?" I nodded. *The Shining* is a book you never really forget. "Quite a few remnants of presidential families here too—descendents of Harrison, Taft, Garfield, and some of Vice President Bush's relatives. Makes for interesting evenings during the winter months."

I asked Hilbert if he was a true year-rounder. "No, not quite," he said. "I teach off-island in the spring but I spend most of the rest of the time here. The fall is ideal for writing. The days are perfect—especially October—this is a typical October day."

And the day was superb; a Riviera light made all the colors sparkle and gave the ocean a silvery sheen. Soft island sounds rolled through the grasses: the distant hum of the island power-generator, the hiss of sea on the cream sands, the purr of electric golfcarts which seemed a favorite form of island transportation, the clink of rigging on the masts of the sailboats.

The fish dock was quiet. Charter boat signs were still evident but the summer crowds were gone. There were strict warnings about the need to obtain shellfish permits from the Wharfinger to dig for quahogs. A note about Dot's Gifthouse and her ceramics, patchworks, jewelry, and driftwood sculptures had become water-stained, and ads for the Allen House (accommodations and meals during the summer) and the Bakery Restaurant were no longer valid. Both were closed for the season.

I followed the narrow road up the northern slopes of Lookout Hill, up through the thick windswept scrub of sumac and bayberry, past a remnant of an old open-topped bus long past its prime, and out onto a windy bluff overlooking Gosnold Pond and the Gosnold monument at the western end of the island. There were no sounds except for the distant rush of the surf on rocky beaches. The dew was still heavy and glistened on the bushes. The path meandered through the thick scrub, full of the fresh aroma of morning. I spotted a rabbit, a large one, just ahead. It saw me too, but didn't pay much attention and resumed its leafy lunch. I walked right up to it and still it continued its nibbling. When I put my hand out to stroke it, the creature stopped eating, gave me a look of annoyance for interrupting its meal and waited for me to withdraw my hand. I did, and it resumed with complete indifference to my presence.

It was then I saw the deer. He must have watched the little incident for there was no fear in the way he stood—in fact there seemed to be a distinct gleam of amusement in his eyes. Having decided I was absolutely harmless, he began advancing toward me, occasionally flicking his magnificent head with its three foot long antlers. I started to back off, and felt rather stupid. He was supposed to back off from *me*—it says so in all the books: *"The deer is a timid creature...."* Fortunately after a few yards he got bored and started nibbling bayberry leaves, and I was able to resume my walk. By the time I arrived back in the village I had seen three full-grown deer, one fawn, two more rabbits, and a snake (the island variety is apparently harmless). I saw my final deer, a beautiful beige doe, enjoying a hearty lunch of chrysanthemums in a garden near the Allen House. Even the high fence, a common sight around many of the village homes, had failed to keep her out.

Memories like these make Cuttyhunk such a special place. There was the old fisherman from Finland, sitting outside his tiny wooden shack shucking clams for a chowder. On one of the tracks leading out of the village was a sign typical of the spirit of the island: YOU ARE NOW ENTERING PRIVATE LANDS. WELCOME. The inhabitants are friendly and seem to enjoy the handful of tourists who arrive daily during the summer to stroll the narrow paths and tan on the beaches. One woman spent half an hour answering my questions about the island's history and even invited me to join her family for dinner.

She was one the year-rounders, a hearty bunch of residents some of whom make a living by doing odd jobs for one another or taking out amateur fishermen to hunt the great bass that run between the Elizabeth Islands. I heard from the ''summerities'' who live here only during the warmer part of the year of the age-old feuds between some of the year-rounders. "It's just like a soap opera," one summerite told me." Every June I come back and I'm hardly off the boat before they start giving me the rundown of winter

A Boat on Cuttyhunk

— this one moved, even on land,
with the rush and boldness
of a wave....

escapades. For the first week my house is never empty. There's always some-one coming in with tales—fantastic tales—about the goings-on here. And they get so serious—there are some families that never speak to one another. Still, what can you expect, it's a tiny place, most of the homes are all bunched up together, and forty people with nothing to do for six months—it's amazing there aren't annual massacres."

The road from the tip of Lookout Hill leads down between neat stone walls to the library and Gosnold Church, with its stumpy white belfry. Narrow paved paths shaded by trees continue on down the slope to the hotel, the school, and the playing field overlooking the boatyard.

And then I was back on the beach again, sunning myself by the side of an enormous rusty buoy and wishing I had another day on this peaceful oasis. Cuttyhunk is a little world unto itself—a tiny patch of sand and sumac. It's not on the New England tourist route, possibly because there's not much to do here except enjoy the peace of its quiet lanes and match wits with the occa-sional deer. There are few cars or trucks because of the absence of paved roads and places to go. Cuttyhunk is what you make of it. If you enjoy your own company, you'll love it.

12. Prudence Island

Narragansett's "Whale in the Bay"

An overused metaphor for islands is the whale: "Like an enormous whale the island rose up," and so forth. In the case of Prudence Island, however, the similarities are unusually marked. This cozy green world, reminiscent of the Maine backwoods, nestles among smaller islets in Narragansett Bay and bears striking resemblance to a whale both in profile and cartological form. They even call it "The Whale in the Bay" and islanders seem to have adopted the whale logo enthusiastically on brochures, house shingles, and even wine labels (yes, Prudence has its very own winery).

Like a whale, Prudence is gentle and playful; it's a place where smiles come easily and life moves along slowly with abundant time for sun-basking and bathing in the ocean. Paved roads provide a bare framework for exploring the seven by two mile island and enormous (whale-like?) autos, most at least two decades old, lollop along on two cylinders without mufflers and shocks. Five times a day when the ferry docks at Homestead they waddle down to the wharf, puffing and steaming, deliver or collect their cargoes, and waddle back again, disappearing like strange forest creatures up dusty tracks to homes deep in the woods.

"No point getting new ones. Sea air'll rust 'em up in a year or less and what d'you need 'em for anyhow?" My informant, one of the island's fifty or so permanent residents, kindly offered me a lift when I arrived on the early morning ferry from Bristol. I wasn't sure where I wanted to go but he took me anyway and became an instant island guide. We passed other islanders in baggy trousers and baseball caps. Wildeyed girls in halters and shorts oggled the ferry visitors looking for friends—or fun.

As we passed Bill Shield's Prudence Inn, the island's only hotel (the name is, of course, inscribed on a whale-shaped sign), my guide pointed across the road to a bedraggled clapboard cottage set back behind a yard littered with rusting cars, vans, and miscellaneous bits of automobile-anatomy scattered in the grass. "That's Welfare Willie's. He's got more autos than just 'bout anyone. None of 'em work, mind you." Further along, dozens of steep lopsided steps climbed up to Edcliff House, a delicate shuttered residence perched

EDCLIFF

Edcliff House
Prudence
Island

on the edge of a cliff-like hill. Then without warning the road rounded a curve and presented us with a steep grade for the next quarter mile. The old Chevy wheezed and thumped and somehow dragged itself over the summit. He laughed "One day she's not going to make it. Then I start looking for my next old lady. I've had five now and they all died right here. That's about the only thing people like to change on Prudence."

We left behind the line of neat cottages between Homestead and Sandy Point (the best beach on the east side) and started across the wooded interior of the island on arrow-straight Broadway. At the schoolhouse, a typical white New England structure complete with belltower, a road on our left went south to a park along the bay. This is one of nine components of The Bay Islands Park, a 2,600 acre recreational area stretching from Conanicut Island at the southern end of the bay to Patience Island and the North Prudence Sanctuary, a mere 12 miles from Providence. The park offers a wide range of water-related environments from forts, beaches, and popular fishing spots, to 56 exclusive acres on a former Newport Ocean Drive estate and isolated sanctuaries where ibis, egrets and heron can be viewed from coves and sandy paths among the dunes. The South Prudence Park has private boat-docking facilities as well as regular ferry services from Providence and Portsmouth, and day-long cruises on the Bay Queen. Visitors here can picnic and camp while exploring the rocky shore, cranberry bogs, and oak forests. Serious fishermen come for the bluefish, and striped bass. Novices make do with the delicious island clams when they can catch them.

My guide dropped me at Prudence Park among a cluster of ornate Victorian summer houses. Out in the bay was the bald rocky dome of Hope Island Sanctuary, one of the most significant nesting centers for large wading birds in the northeast. No visitors are allowed here during the April 15-July 31 nesting season but guided tours are organized in late summer and fall.

A dusty track led alongside the ocean for a mile or so. It was a hot August day and I was glad of the water bottle in my back pocket. My trunks were in the car at Bristol but I found a secluded cove with a tiny strip of beach and skinny-dipped while seagulls circled overhead, apparently unfamiliar with such antics. The remnants of a cooked lobster and crisp roll from Marcy Dunbar's store at Homestock Dock (one of only two stores on the island) made a perfect informal lunch. I had the place all to myself.

A little later on, company would have been most welcome. I continued north along the sandy road to the tidal flats which separate North Prudence from the rest of the island. Ten miles of narrow trails here lead through a land-

The "Old Road" – Prudence

scape of dunes and coves, hedges, and old walls that once marked the boundaries of farms, long abandoned. Small rounded hills, covered in oak and pitch pine, mingle with salt marshes full of bird sounds and watery scurryings in the rushes.

A crude hand-painted sign read: THIS WAY TO DESERT, so I followed a path south through the woods. The air was motionless under the trees and even strands of tiny ants carrying their burdens of twiglets and bits of leaves seemed to be moving unusually slowly in the heat. One or two large biting flies tried Kamikaze dives at exposed limbs but even they seemed to tire of the game as I climbed higher up the sandy slope and out onto a bleak mini-Gobi of golden dunes. Some were quite substantial, 50 or 60 feet high, and one looked much the same as all the others. I'd hoped for views out across the island but all I could see was shimmering sand in all directions. Normally my orientation is excellent. This time it vanished completely and within a few minutes I was hopelessly lost, parading up and down dunes like an abandoned legionnaire. This is when I could have done with company but all I had was the silence, the shimmering heat, and no shade. I made a rough guess at south and kept a straight line for half a mile or so across the dunes right into Prudence Swamp. Fortunately the hot summer had evaporated much of the water and I managed to skirt around the edge without losing my boots in a bog. I did however discover the lethal tendrils of the Bullbriar, which from a distance resembles bright green ivy but on closer acquaintance rips and tears at clothes and flesh with stiletto thorns.

Bloody and somewhat disheartened I stopped by a stream for a drink and a washing of wounds. Luck was with me and I discovered a path leading through arches of trees. Silky grasses rustled together by crumbling stone walls and from my map I recognized this as an old island highroad which once linked the scores of small farms on Prudence, now all overgrown and returned to nature.

Then by sheer chance came the winery. The forest ended abruptly at the edge of a small valley on the leeside of a hill. A Wyeth-flavored farmhouse sat on top of the hill overlooking 16 acres of meticulously pruned vines surrounded by fences to keep out the island deer, now said to number over 200.

My reception at the farm could not have been more gracious. Bill and Natalie Bacon welcomed me into their large kitchen with its stone fireplace and broad oak table. One glance at my bedraggled state and they offered me their bathroom, then a jug of ice cold water and chunks of cheese. From the

Bill Bacon
—winemaker

windows I could see in every direction over the island. Their son, the local schoolteacher, described Prudence's long history, starting with its purchase from the Narragansett Indians by Roger Williams in 1637. Even this secluded haven did not survive the ravages of the British during the Revolution. In 1776 a Captain Wallace and 250 armed men landed here and destroyed every home they could find along with barns and crops. From the way Natalie looked while her son told the tale, the incident might have happened last year. Seven generations of her family, the Chases, have lived on the island. They came originally from Manchester, England and, interestingly, a dozen of Wallace's men were from the same city.

We began the inevitable wine-tasting. Bill only produces two kinds of wine—a pleasantly fruity Gamay Beaujolais and a crisp, flinty white Pinot Chardonnay which cut through my system like ice and brought a healthy tingle to all extremities. Bill called it "a bit spritzy." We must have "tasted" two whole bottles, if not three, while the plump, pink-faced couple recounted the secrets of their wine-making. The grapes they chose are hardy varietals, although, according to Bill, they'd never been troubled by frost and never lost a harvest. "Wouldn't be no problem if we did, these are special stock with three buds. If you lose one, they grow another." Natalie loved the wild island grapes, the "foxy" kind often used in New York State wines. "Makes me think it's September when I eat them. When I was a little kid I used to go to school with these two boys and in September our recess was sitting on the stone wall by the classroom popping grapes into our mouths non-stop till the bell went—we called it our September wine."

Reluctantly I had to catch the last ferry back to Bristol. Bill offered me a lift in his worn VW and we crashed along island backroads past the winery cellars, down the long slope from the farm, with me clutching two bottles of white Chardonnay complete with Prudence whales on the labels.

We made it with only minutes to spare and I scrambled aboard just in time to watch us cast off and start the short, calm journey back to the mainland. The sun was low, silhouetting the island deep purple in the sunset. Seagulls circled after us as we edged around the lighthouse at Hog Island, another quiet little backwater in the bay which gets by quite happily without electricity and other unnecessary modernizations. The refined waterfront mansions of Bristol, perched on lawns sloping into the bay, glowed gold and pink in the evening's last light; a family of ducks quacked a welcome as we eased against the pier.

13. Smith Island

The Right Tight Isles

Crisfield, embarkation point for Smith and Tangier Islands in Chesapeake Bay, calls itself (with unusual Southern immodesty) the "Crab Capital of the World." And if the summertime aroma of steaming crabs is anything to go by, this little town, sprawled on its promontory overlooking the bay, deserves its reputation. Crabs are everywhere. The sidewalks, the docks, the parking lots, are littered with scatterings of red shell and claw bits; piles of crab pots give off a pungent smell of old bait; seagulls fight over remnants and sparrows peck at discarded legs for overlooked meat morsels. Steam billows from the crab-picking plants by the piers, where deftly-fingered women pry out the claw meat, the "special," and the highly-valued backfin from prime "Jimmies" and "Sooks" (mature male and female crabs), while big-bicepted men shovel new loads of freshly steamed crabs onto the table in front of each picker.

"This is what s'all about." Rudy Thomas snapped off the backfin from a bright scarlet crab and offered me the snowy pile of flesh. "You'd go far to find anything taste so good as this little piece of Blue." I sucked the meat off the cartilage for that combination taste of salt spray and creamy-textured seafood. "Clawmeat's good too, bit stronger tastin' than special but backfin's the real stuff—that's what makes your best crab cakes and crab balls and your Crab Imperial."

He pointed to the upper terrace of the Sidestreet Seafood Market adjoining the picking plant, where a dozen tourists sat on picnic tables hammering crabs and extracting the meat in frustratingly small pieces. "I been eatin' crab since I was weaned and I never got tired. I see them up there crackin' shells and, I tell you, give me five, ten minutes spare and I'd be up there with 'em everytime."

I was deep in crab country. Although the winter season brings oysters by the thousands of bushels to Crisfield the men think of themselves primarily as crabbers and discuss the qualities of their pots and tiny shallow-draught workboats as lovingly as their own children. The only problem is that it's very difficult to understand the conversations, especially those of the Tangier

Islanders whose rich brogue, full of extended "a's" and "o's," is reminiscent of their English heritage and the long slow drawl of Cornish fishermen. I even had problems with Rudy. He is skipper of the Tangier Island mailboat and regular contact with outsiders has mellowed his accent somewhat, but as he exclaimed about the glories of crabs and crabbing, it became thicker and richer so that I found myself merely guessing at meanings.

"You won't have so much problem with people on Smith," he assured me, trying hard to suppress the eccentricities of his accent. " They've had more contact with the mainland, so they don't talk so strange as we do on Tangier."

My plan was to go to Smith Island first and then Tangier, but there was time to kill before the 12:30 p.m. ferry from Somers Cove Marina and Rudy had offered to act as guide. We paused at the softshell packing plant near the main docks where lines of leg-weary women stood washing, cleaning, clipping, and sorting the green-gray creatures ready for freezing and transport to the elegant tables of restaurants up and down the east coast.

"This is where the real money is. Hardshells you perhaps make $12 or so a bushel, that's about four dozen crabs, but softshells you get much more, and they're real popular right now too. But it's hard—it's 24 hour work watchin' them in the tanks. Waiting for them to shed. You got to watch for all the signs. Most look for the little signs on the belly and legs and keep shiftin' them from tank to tank dependin' on where the signs are and what color they are. You've got to work fast too—you've only got an hour or so after they've shed before they start hardenin' again. You've got to get them out of water and pack 'em up good in seaweed or straw so they don't get bruised and ship 'em fast over here for clippin' or freezin'. You've got to keep 'em alive till you clean 'em, too, or they'll go off fast."

We strolled past piles of boxes filled with writhing green crabs. They look identical to hards until you touch them and feel the soft shell buckle under finger-pressure.

"There's nothin' better'n softshells. You just boil 'em up a bit first to tender 'em and then fry 'em in butter, maybe with a little crab seasoning, maybe not, dependin' on taste, an' you've got one of the best dinners y'ever had."

I asked Rudy if he'd ever thought of being a crabman.

"Oh, it's too late for me now. You've gotta start young—real young—I couldn't do it, because I've not been doin' it. Y'often have to run 25, 30 miles just lookin' for a few pots, 'specially in the spring. Crabs go south as the water gets warmer. Y'have to go way down off Cape Charles and Norfolk to find 'em. That's about a three hour run before y'even start fishin' up the pots."

A Workboat from Smith

"But that's when they make it good; when the crabs start gettin' up this way everybody's out catchin' them and the price goes down specially with the young ones fishin' round 450 pots—and they pick 'em up—gaffin', heavin', cullin', draggin' out sea-nettles and rebaitin'—every one of 'em—every day. 'Course they got hydraulic rigs an' all now but it's still damned hard work—up at three, four o'clock in the morning and out in all kinds of weather for 12 hours, maybe longer. Heck—there's lots better jobs around than crabbin!''

As ferry departure time approached I wandered to the marina past the Captain's Galley restaurant (famous for creamy crab cakes), past Bradshaw's Hardware Store, past the miniature Greek temple-styled Bank of Crisfield (now a small museum), past the barber's shop with all the familiar feel of a Hopper painting. The town seems to have changed little since its heyday as a rail head when the railroad ran down the middle of the street. Today there's a long grass strip along what must be one of the widest main streets in the USA. Even with all the summer tourists, the place has a dozing appearance; only the new marina complex is evidence of contemporary renaissance.

A plump, smiling Alan Tyler welcomes passengers aboard the *Captain Tyler* ferry and immediately launches into a description of the seafood lunch being offered at the Bayside Inn over on Smith Island: "Now they do you real fine over there—you eat all you want of crab soup, real Smith Island crab soup with big chunks of backfin, crab cakes—some of the best you'll ever taste—clam fritters, baked ham, corn pudding, homemade macaroni salad, and stewed tomatoes, vegetables, cole slaw, rolls, and as much fresh fruit pie as you can manage.''

Mouths water and eyes glaze at the prospects of tables laden with island delicacies and the journey seems too long as Alan slowly eases his 65 foot boat across the silver waters of the bay. Some of the crabbing work boats are returning to the harbor after eight or nine hours hauling pots. Two miles out a haze settles around the ferry; black cormorants skim the smooth ocean and vanish in crisp dives, emerging much later with lunch already half eaten. Passengers relax in the peaceful nowhereness and even a gang of boisterous children seem calmed by the hypnotic journey. Then someone spots the island, a faint gray blur on the horizon, and we all peer into the stillness, mouths watering once again at the prospects of lunch ahead.

The eight-by-ten mile expanse of Smith Island is actually three islands, each with its own tight-knit community. The total population barely exceeds 600. Early explorers rejoiced in these flat marshy wildernesses filled with wildfowl and surrounded by bay waters teeming with oysters, crabs, and fish. Captain John Smith eased his way up the Chesapeake in 1608 and recorded in his typically enthusiastic manner that: "Heaven and earth seemed never to have agreed better for man's commodious and delightful habitation."

Settlers who scurried here in the mid 1800s as dissenters from Lord Baltimore's Colony in St. Mary's County, Maryland, originated from Cornwall, England. Their family names of Tyler, Marshall, Bradshaw and Evans still predominate today. Their accents were thick, their dialect contained many of the ancient words of the Cornish language, and their social habits were distinctly anarchistic. Smith (or The Right Tight Isles as the settlers called their new home) rapidly developed a reputation for lawlessness, violence, and drunkenness. Scratching a living from the sandy land and the ocean was a far less profitable and a much more arduous business than today. The islanders worked hard and from all accounts played hard. Family feuding was not uncommon and there were occasional skirmishes with residents of Tangier Island, who claimed equal rights to the vast oyster beds in the bay. Snooping government officials received equally stern treatment, particularly when they attempted to restrict the islanders' freedom to shoot ducks and geese with their deadly seven foot long "swivel guns" that fired two pounds of shot, capable of killing or maiming scores of fowl at a time.

It took the powerful bible-thumping Reverend Joshua Thomas, "The Parson of the Isles," to convert the errant populace to strict Methodism. They were particularly impressed with his threats of hellfire and damnation and his courage when preaching to the British army based on Tangier Island immediately prior to the 1814 battle for Fort McHenry in Baltimore. He forecasted their rout and was proved right the following day; since then the islanders have remained loyal worshippers at the three Methodist churches on the island.

"You're either Methodist or alcoholic," said Alan Tyler with his boyish, rabbit-tooth grin. "That's about all the choice you got here." One of the passengers said he'd been told the island was distinctly dry, to which Alan replied with a droll, "Oh it is, it is. On my, it is."

After an hour or so at sea, we approached the first of the island communities, Tylerton, up a long narrow channel, past a lonely hunting clubhouse set in reeds. Egrets and white heron patrolled the shallows and paused to watch warily as the *Captain Tyler* eased by with hardly a ripple. A wooden sign stuck in the marsh at the edge of the channel warned: "Don't Forget God,

Rhodes Point
– Smith Island

He Won't Forget You." Ahead we could see scatterings of crab shacks, little white sheds at the end of long rickety piers. Some were lopsided, sinking slowly into the mud; others were a crisp white bordered by long lines of water tanks for sorting the soft-shell crabs. The workboats were back early from the bay and the catch was being hauled onto the docks, dozens of bushel baskets of kicking and squirming creatures.

Our boat moved slowly past the tiny village of 150 inhabitants with its stubby-towered church and scattering of white clapboard homes. A plump woman walked down the dock pushing a cart full of empty baskets; other equally plump crabmen's wives were gathered along the harbor edge. Two of them waved. The passengers seemed delighted to be noticed and waved back. One little boy said he thought all the waving was silly and received a sharp rebuke from his mother, who proceeded to wave his hand for him while he stood on one leg, not sure whether to giggle or burst into tears.

I was with Alan in the wheel house. "Tylerton's a nice little place. People keep to themselves a bit but they're friendly enough when they get to know you. We don't stop here but if you stay—there's a couple of tourist homes, try Frances Kitching's place—you'll be able to get the mailboat or one of the workboats to take you. There's always someone going over. Just give them a bit of change and they'll be fine. While back you'd've been able to see Paul—Paul Marshall—carvin' his duck decoys—they call it counter-feitin'—but he's been taken ill so he's stopped doin' it for now."

From Tylerton we followed the channel past more crab shacks and another godly sign to a smaller harbor at Rhodes Point. A line of houses ran parallel to the channel. The village had a clean, fresh look; the inhabitants obviously cared for their small properties and sparkling white fences surrounded neat gardens. We docked by a much larger boat also owed by Alan and used for the annual federally-sponsored seeding of "spat" oysters in key sites across the bay.

"For those having lunch, just go straight across to the Bayside. They're waiting for you." Alan smiled as he watched everyone scamper over to the restaurant. "I do a pretty good commercial," he chuckled.

And a fair one. Lunch was all we had hoped for, with far too many crab cakes and fritters, much too much Virginia ham, and enormous fruit pies for dessert. Slowly and sleepily visitors left the dining room to explore Rhodes Point. A little while later Alan piled most of us into a creaking blue bus and took us for a grand tour along the island's only road, a sinuous mile-and-a-half strip linking Rhodes Point with Ewell, the "capital" of Smith Island, and by far the most appealing of the three communities.

"This road was only built a few years back. 'Fore that there wasn't much contact between the two villages and people got around mainly on bikes. But—when you get a road, you get cars, and my God, we've had our share of cars on Smith!" He pointed at the marsh on either side of the bus. Literally hundreds of abandoned cars, trucks, and buses (482 at last count) have been left to rot in the elements. Gasps of horror! How could such an eyesore have been permitted in such a tranquil place?

"Problem is," Alan told us, "Cars and trucks don't last out here. Salt air gets into every little pore and pretty soon your fancy Ford's fallin' apart at the seams. My last truck—brand new and all sealed—lasted only two years. And there are so many you can't just park 'em in your back yard. So they bring 'em out and this is what you get. State's been plannin' to do something for years. Just last week twenty-five people came on a junket from Annapolis. Twenty five congressmen and god knows who else—all comin' to decide what to do. Y'ask me it'll be a while 'fore anthing happens!"

Shaded under large maples and sycamores, Ewell greeted us, prim as a pin, with trim lawns and gardens edged by fences and hedges; everywhere there was a sense of communal pride and shared values. I decided to stay and arranged to meet Alan the following day for the return trip to the mainland (such an impromptu decision during the summer season is not always possible; advance reservations are usually necessary).

As the blue bus trundled away I strolled the shady lanes in search of Frances Kitching's house. For years now this determined, no-nonsense lady has provided a few guest rooms for visitors who want more than a two-hour peep at island life. She was in the garden pruning bushes and seemed a little put out by my arrival.

"It's just you is it?" She didn't seem very thrilled at the prospect. "I wasn't expecting anybody." I must have looked forlorn, weighed down with heavy cameras and overnight bags, and her frown quickly became a grin, wrinkling a deeply-tanned face. "C'mon, I'll show you your room."

Just what I'd expected too, chintzy and cozy with small bedside lamps in lacy shades and pictures of island beauty spots on the wall. "Dinner's at 5:00 p.m., prompt. D'you know where you're going?" Sensible question. After ten minutes advice from Frances I'd developed an exhaustive itinerary.

I think of all island communities visited during my journeys for this book, Ewell is my favorite; I love its winding lanes, its oyster shell tracks leading off into hammocks of eucalyptus and pine; I love the shady main street dotted

The Great Tabernacle — Ewell

with white Victorian cottages, the Leroy Evans and Sons general store which is a focus for island gossip, the Pitchcroft Restaurant serving more eat-all-you-can lunches to travelers taking the mailboat ferry to Ewell, the quaint round-walled artesian wells pumping fresh water from 1,200 feet down under the bay. And I love the bold antics of "shrikes" (small tern-like birds that seem to enjoy nipping exposed toes and ankles), the little grassy paths to the crab shacks where the crabmen find moments of ease after hours on the ocean, and the small family burial plots in the gardens of island homes.

I passed the Methodist church with its raised tombs, a traditional form of island burial. Behind, in a field, was the old gray tabernacle where islanders hold their annual summer camp meeting, a revivalist celebration of hymns, readings, and preachings, which brings the populace of the three villages together for a week of worship, fine eating, and fun. One elderly resident I met near the church, one of the numerous Evanses in the community, thought things weren't lively enough anymore. "There used to be shoutin', lots of shoutin' when I was a girl. And testifyin'—oh my Lord the testifyin' we had—amazing tales you heard, 'nough to keep you straight in the Lord for 'nother year at least. And the people—it was filled with people, youngsters—everybody. The cemetery was full of flowers too—all over. Now the young ones seem more bothered 'bout the dancin' at night than the preachin'; don't seem so good as it used to be. Maybe it's me, I don't know."

According to Reverend Joshua Thomas the meetings were "wonderful manifestations." "No scene in this sinful world," he enthused, "could surpass the moral grandeur of these meetings where all would be singing joyfully the songs of Zion or shouting over their children and friends, newly born of God. They shouted all over the ground, and many fell and lay as dead on the earth. Whey they recovered they began to praise God wonderfully!"

Things keep changing on Smith. Now there are microwave transmitters for the local telephone system, video games in Marshall's store, where the older crabmen still sit in semi-permanent council; there are crackling staccatto motor bikes, an over-profusion of unmufflered and unlicensed autos, portable tape decks, and most alarming of all, the gradual disappearance of "fast" land as ocean erosion takes its toll.

"A hundred years from now there won't be much here," Frances told me as I returned for dinner at 5:00 p.m. (prompt). Normally when her guest house is full she offers a family-style dinner similar to lunch at the Bayside, but that night I enjoyed a superb crab chowder, three golden-sauteed soft shell crabs, and slices of apple cake with cream. We talked into the evening about island life and traditions. "We're not that unusual y'know. People come expecting I don't know what, thinking we perhaps haven't discovered air conditioning or television yet or still light up kerosene lamps after sunset. You have to laugh. One woman— someone who should have known better—thought she'd have to go outside to the toilet."

In her spare time Frances worked on a book about island life which contains a selection of her favorite and famed recipes, including the perfect crab cake preparation, oyster pie, crab Creole, deep fried "Buckrams" (soft shell crabs with shells slightly hardened to paper texture), Crab Imperial, various wild fowl and clam dishes, plus ways of serving the Chesapeake "manos" (softshell clams loved by New Englanders but still considered suspect by local watermen), and such delicious concoctions as Peach Pie and Hot Milk Cake. Frances has great respect for her island neighbors. "They work hard, really hard. There's no welfare on Smith—not like some of those other places up north—people just don't want it. If someone's in trouble—if they've been ill or lost a boat or something equally bad—everybody chips in to help. They're close—my blessed, are they close!"

I was curious what islanders did for recreation.

"Hunting used to be real popular in the fall, for ducks and geese out in the marsh, but now they leave most of it to outsiders, people who come in and use the club. Muskrats used to be popular, too, for eating, but you don't see many now. A day out from crabbing or oystering costs plenty—it's an expensive way to enjoy yourself. Some people—some of the older ones—like to collect Indian things, arrowheads and bits n' pieces. Th' island's full of them—it was a real popular place with Indians. And the women, well they do what their mothers and grandmothers used to do—canning and preserving—there's so much fruit on Smith, wild figs and pomegranates and people love their fruit trees in the backyards. And then there's the old heads at the store playing dominoes and pinochle and pitch. They spend hours at it of an evening—and yarn spinning, that still goes on. They've heard the tales a hundred times but you get someone like Alex Kellam start on and you've just got to listen right to the end."

The young have their own nightly rituals, the almost European-styled promenading up and down the main street, pausing at the snack bar near the school, showing off the latest in whining mopeds and souped-up autos. "They've got to get rid of all that go somewhere, somehow," Frances explained solemnly as motorcycles crackled past her garden. "They're good kids mostly. We don't need police out here. People know how to behave—even the wild one's don't stay wild too long. On islands you learn to be tolerant of others; you have to be or you won't last"

The next day I rambled around Ewell stroking the cats that seem to be everywhere, pausing to chat with the old watermen watching over their molting crabs out on the rickety piers. I sat in the shade of the huge maple on Pitchcroft, near the grave of a British soldier who died from wounds received in the Baltimore battle more than a century-and-a-half ago. People passed, smiling, while I sketched.

Later on I got a lift out on a workboat to Tylerton and spent an hour or so exploring the narrow streets and peeping into the windows of Paul Marshall's decoy workshop. A young boy offered me a trip back in his speedboat and we raced along past thickets of reeds, sending herons flapping gawkily into a perfect blue sky.

The slow content of island life seeped in. I abandoned lists and itineraries, I banished the little "what next" demon, and let time roll along easily until Alan Tyler's blue bus creaked back into Ewell, full of crabcake-cushioned travelers.

Reluctantly, very reluctantly, I left Smith. My only compensation was the prospect of more islands, more unknown places, ahead. And that made me happy.

14. Tangier Island

Soft-Shell Serendipity

The *Steven Thomas* eased out of Crisfield harbor into a silver morning haze with the scream of seagulls and the hiss of foam from the bow.

Rudy Thomas, my early morning companion and guide to the crab plants in Crisfield, now wore his captain's cap. He peered into the mists trying to avoid the crab pot buoys scattered like confetti across Chesapeake Bay. It was not the kind of ride he enjoyed and he stood quietly at the wheel while a group of good ol' boys from the island gurgled together in their rich, robust dialect, unintelligible to most eavesdroppers, myself included. Rudy winked. "It's not worth translatin'—all wives and girls and Saturday night talk. You've heard it before."

After an hour and a quarter in limbo the island emerged slowly from the silvery grayness. Tourist passengers tensed, cameras and binoculars ready. Even the handful of residents paused briefly in their conversations to watch the spindly piers and white crab shacks drift by. The stumpy church tower was our beacon and we headed right for it, sliding gently into dock, watched by a bunch of old salts.

It certainly seems a tiny place (and getting smaller as pieces slowly disappear into the bay), but that doesn't worry the Tangiermen. They're much more concerned about their immediate livelihood, crabbing. Similar to most other bay regions, the island has developed its own specialty, which, as gourmets well know, is the softshell crab. Actually it shares its reputation with Smith Island, but because of the long Virginia open season, Tangier has a higher catch record than any other locality in the bay. It is equally well known for winter "hard" crabs, caught by its dredger fleet. Yet at times visitors would hardly suspect that such a prolific industry exists here. During the day the harbor is calm; dinghies bob and bump against the wooden jetties, crab shacks are empty, groups of crab pounds lie still in the water. But early in the morning, before dawn, is a different matter. Then the village is filled with the racket of crackling engines as the host of little boats move into the bay; late in the afternoon when they return there's a similar din as piles of bushel baskets filled with writhing, clicking, bubble-blowing blue crabs are unloaded.

Most tourists never see this sight, unless, of course, they stay overnight at Crockett's Chesapeake House. The majority only come for a couple of hours. But even they leave a little quieter in spirit, a little more relaxed, and possibly a little envious too.

This is still an idyllic place. Even though recent modernizations, including the widening of main street to a gross 10 feet, have introduced some insensitive visual elements, life still continues much the way it did when the original settlers arrived in the seventeenth century.

"They were a hardy lot, those early Cornish families—the Crocketts, Pruitts, Parkses, and Dizes." A charming lady, Mrs. Clarke, met travelers at the dock and offered her services as guide as she led us to (an optional) lunch at Chesapeake House. Walking backwards the whole distance (a remarkable feat), Mrs. Clarke gave us succinct and amusing snippets of island history while pointing out landmarks and Tangier characters.

Although discovered by Captain John Smith in 1608, nothing much happened to this "fruitful and delightful land" until 1666, when a Mr. West journeyed from the Virginia mainland, purchased the island from local Indians for "two fine overcoats," and used it as a stock raising farm. Then twenty years later John Crockett bought a substantial portion of the island from West and proceeded to populate it with members of Cornish families from southwest England. They brought their skills as fishermen, boat builders, and farmers, and their thick Cornish dialect full of long "ois" and "aahs," very similar to that still heard today on the Outer Banks of North Carolina.

Although records are somewhat scarce, it appears life on this isolated patch of marsh 12 miles from the mainland was characterized by a considerable degree of licentious living, as was the case with nearby Smith Island. But in 1804, along came Joshua Thomas in his boat, *The Methodist,* bringing his great Bible full of lurid descriptions of the dreadful penalties awaiting sinful residents of the islands. The bounding enthusiasm and stamina of this "Parson of the Isles" impressed the population, and in 1814, when he prayed with memorable results for the British defeat at Fort McHenry, he became the undoubted spiritual leader of Chesapeake Bay.

Tangier remains a devoutly religious community. Work on Sundays of any kind is still frowned upon and church attendance is expected of everyone. Liquor of course is virtually nonexistent, and many of the small handwritten notices of forthcoming events found on store bulletin boards reflect the spiritual interests of the residents:

Main Street. Tangier

Church attendance is down again—C'mon!

"The Gospel of Jesus in Song" on Friday—Don't miss it.

Special Sunday School. Everybody welcome. Please come on.

The Gospel Boys Group is coming at last—Should be a great show!

The island possesses a great sense of family unity. Until recently many front and back yards were used as private burial grounds. If you study the headstones you'll notice some unusual first names—Beaulah, Asbury, Sophronia, Dixie, Homer, Venie, and Pettie.

Main street, sometimes known as King Street, is still a delight in spite of the widening and replacement of white picket fences by chicken wire contraptions. We doglegged around the Methodist church and strolled slowly towards lunch past high roofed houses, late Victorian in style, all gleaming white behind neat lawns. Golf carts, a popular form of island transport, hummed past; cars are considered rather redundant. The occasional scooter crackled out across the marshes which lay green and smooth behind the houses. They look peaceful enough, although summer turns them into a rampant breeding ground for biting insects—green flies, gnats, mosquitoes, and sheep flies.

"They can be a real nuisance," Mrs. Clarke (still walking backward) told us. "They rise earlier than most places, too. You can get eaten up at six in the morning if you're not sprayed. The watermen pay 'em no mind though and we've got purple martins to feed on 'em—but there's still plenty left for the likes of all you."

We passed Nice's Cafe, (crabcakes and softshell crab sandwiches), the store which doubles as the island museum, and Vernon Bradshaw's studio filled with his own lively paintings and sketches of island life. He opens up when he feels like it. Today the place was closed.

"He could be out duck-hunting but more'n likely he's off with his brushes somewhere. He's his own man—like most of the Tangier folk. They stick to their ways and don't get too much affected by comers-in."

Duck was about the only dish not served at the gargantuan family-style lunch in the dining room of Chesapeake House. Like the Smith islanders, the 800 residents here enjoy their fare and it shows in their generous waistlines and rotund faces. Forty or so guests got a taste of island food as we sat down to an eat-all-you-can banquet of crab cakes, clam fritters, baked ham, corn pudding, cole slaw, peas, pickled beets, potato salad, apple puree, hot rolls, pound cake, and iced tea.

Golf carts with dainty fringed tops waited outside to provide the traditional one dollar tour. Six of us piled into one of them and we glided down the rest of King Street, then turned into the marshes and over the humpbacked bridge across "Big Gut Canal" which divides the island. It was hot, with hardly a breeze. Our driver was a jolly young housewife who still seemed as intrigued as we were by Tangier.

"We've really got everything we need here—honestly. We recently got a microwave telephone service and cable TV. We get our water from wells—all of them are more than 1000 feet deep. We've got a post office, a fire department, a school—all 12 grades too—a new indoor recreation center, one policeman, a visiting nurse, a city council, and our very own mayor. What else d'you need except good weather, good kids, and plenty of crabs. And we've got all those too!"

"Looks peaceful don'it?" our guide asked and her passengers nodded wistfully. "Well 'tis really. There's not much trouble at all. Worse thing is when we get hit by a storm—then you know how lonely y'are out here. There was a terror back in 1933—they called it th' August Storm—it put th' whole place under water. Some of these houses were flooded up to their bedrooms. Most people lost just about ev'thing they owned. The crab shacks were wiped out pretty much. It took years to get ev'thing right again. Some said we wouldn't make it."

She smiled proudly at her tiny world set in the blue infinities of the bay. "Still one of the nicest places don't y' think?"

More envious nods from the passengers.

I disembarked at the Methodist church and wandered among the piers and shacks around the ferry dock. Cats slid among broken crab pots picking at bits of shells for scraps of meat. Seagulls stood like sentinels on the pilings waiting for the boats to return littered with bait and discarded remnants from the raised crab pots.

Crabbing is a fascinating world unto itself. It has its own phraseology. Crabbers refer to the "first rush" (spring); to "reading" (understanding) crabs, and to crabs that "hang up" (die), usually when shedding. Crabs themselves are given all kinds of names, depending on their sex and maturity—there are number ones, Jimmies, she-crabs, snots, sooks, whales, slabs, punks, peelers, shedders, lemon bellies, ballies, and busted sooks. Then, of course,

Tangier Island — on a sleepy summer afternoon

there are the boats: skipjacks, bugeyes, dinkies, Jenkins' creekers, bar cats, mano boats, and Hooper-Island draketails.

Softshells have their own molting terminology too—greens, white signs, pink signs, red signs, ranks, busters, and buckrams. Every waterman can read the subtle signs of molting. Some are immediately apparent. "White-sign" crabs have a thin rim of white on the crab's swimming leg which indicates that there are around two weeks more before shedding. Other colors are equally accurate indicators of the process.

Dinnertime came too soon at Chesapeake House. The day-visitors had left around 4 p.m., as the workboats chugged in from the bay. I decided to stay overnight and by 7 p.m. found myself, along with four other guests, tackling yet one more of those enormous help-yourself meals. This time I was less ambitious and found I could walk comfortably around the village as the light went down behind the marshes. The young people were out promenading up King Street, showing off on their bikes, sharing sodas at the two snack bars and whispering together by the post office. Two elderly watermen stood by the school watching the sun drop into the bay and agreeing sadly, in their rich Tangier dialect, that tomorrow would be a "Bluebird Day"—a warm cloudless day, ideal for visitors but useless for duck hunting.

Down by the dock I strolled along oyster shell paths and listened to the water lapping against the tarred pilings. Oysters are scarce now in the Chesapeake because of the devastating effect of the MSX disease caused by polluted water. It may be decades before the poor hauls improve. Many watermen, who used to spend the winter with their oyster dredges, don't bother anymore. Fortunately crab catches have been good, so many enjoy a few weeks in warmer climes instead, resting up for the spring.

I had intended to rise very early to see the crabmen leave on their 4 a.m. journey into the bay. However, I slept long and deep, made a valiant effort at the huge buffet breakfast, and walked up King Street for the last time to catch the 8 a.m. mailboat back to Crisfield.

The same bunch of old salts who had watched the *Steven Thomas* arrive the previous day were here again, sipping coffee under the awning of the dock and talking of crabs and catches. The postmaster brought the mail, two brown sacks; someone untied the rope and we were off into the crisp air leaving the church, the stick-like piers, and the tiny white crab shacks behind us in the early morning mists.

Back into silver limbo again.

Where the
'softs' become
soft
—Tangier Island.

15. Ocracoke Island

"The Goodliest Land"

Most travelers were turning round at Hatteras and heading north, back up the thin strand of dunes, grass, and marshlands known as the Outer Banks.

I wasn't. I was going on south and waiting for the free ferry to take me across the Hatteras Inlet to Ocracoke Island. And that was just fine. The weather was warm, temperatures in the 80s, the breeze moist but without the hot-shower humidity of Georgia. A perfect day for a seacrossing.

I was lucky. Four days earlier poor Ocracoke had been whipped by 70 mph winds and high tides six feet above normal. The island's only road, linking the town at the southern end with the Hatteras ferry, was cut by miles of drifting sand which buried it to a depth of five feet in places, and by short-lived lagoons which stranded even the most intrepid drivers. Eventually the mess was cleared and the ferries re-started, but it was a sober reminder to residents and travelers of the tenuous existence of these thread-thin banks. Lines of dunes can vanish overnight, streams change courses, beaches change shape. Even the editor of the *Ocracoke Island News* sounded panicky: "What will happen during the next storm? Will the pounding waves of the ocean reach the highway next time? Or will this segment of road be washed out totally? The building of sand dunes seems futile—the ocean only washes them back down again. Who will take responsibiltiy for dealing with this problem?"

Ultimately the elements will resolve the problem. The ocean and the wind love to dally with these strips of sand, moving them backwards and forwards, cutting new channels through them, taking from one place and making new land somewhere else. The National Parks Department, the Corps of Engineers, and a score of little townships will try to understand the problems and solve them but, in the end, the elements will have their way.

It feels wild here. I traveled from the ferry dock on Ocracoke Island, down highway 12, to the little town scattered around circular Silver Lake at the southern tip—eighteen miles along a narrow ribbon of sand and low dunes covered with sea oats and marram grass. Most of the way I could only see flickers of ocean on either side, a rolling surf on the seaweed edge hissing over cream beaches; quieter lagoon-like waters of Pamlico Sound on the inland side fringed by marshes and curls of scrub-covered bars. A "wilderness of sand, surf, and solitude" to quote one local poet, a place for long silent walks and quiet contemplations among the barrier dunes.

Even Blackbeard loved the place and had a house built here. According to local traditions up and down the east coast the devilish pirate with the ribbons in his beard spent so much time burying treasure on isolated islets from Florida to Maine, it's remarkable he ever had time for actual looting and piracy. But he seemed to have had a special affection for Ocracoke (or Nokokon or Wococock or Oakocock depending on the date of the map—spelling was not a particularly important facet of cartography in those early days). His feelings were apparently shared by many other pirates who found this an ideal place to repair damaged ships, recover from strange illnesses, and await the passage of Spanish galleons fat with gold and jewels from the Americas. "Calico Jack" Rackam visited a number of times with his throat-slashing moll, Ann Bonney, and her equally blood-thirsty companion, Mary Read. Then came Big Jim Braham, Otway Burns, Charles Vane and Joe Lawson, all privateers, who enjoyed the island's seclusion in the latter part of the 18th century.

Blackbeard, otherwise known as Edward Teach, met his match here in the form of the intrepid Lieutenant Robert Maynard who neatly lopped off his head, ribbons and all, in a sword fight, after capturing Teach's ship *The Adventure* on November 22, 1718. The pirate's headless body—so the legend goes—was then immediately thrown overboard whereupon it proceeded to swim around the ship seven times before sinking to the bottom. A less flamboyant tale has him decently buried on firm ground and, in fact, an oversized skeleton, complete with brass buttons and pirate-like trinkets, was once found north of the village.

History seems to have made a very distinct mark on this isolated string of sand dunes way out in the Atlantic. Few people realize that it was here and not at Roanoke that the Sir Walter Raleigh expedition under Captain Lane first disembarked on June 23, 1585. This was only a brief pause though, and the island slumbered on until the early 1700s when the colonial assembly recognized its trading potentials and approved it as a station for pilots to guide ships through the hazardous shoals of Ocracoke Inlet. Pilot lore and the descendents of pilot families still shape the island's story, although there have been times when it looked as if that story might be rather brief.

One occasion was a vicious raid by Spaniards from St. Augustine in 1747 when they killed several residents, burned ships, slaughtered livestock, and generally had themselves a fine foray. But there was retribution four years later when three Spanish ships were beached in a terrible storm and the "bankers" found themselves knee-deep in silver and pieces-of-eight. Unfortunately, the colonial government made sure that most of the wealth was returned, but tales of chests lost in the sands here have fascinated visitors and residents for decades.

During the Revolution, the British were as anxious as the Spanish to see the little trading town, "this contemptible port," destroyed. Apparently the Ocracoke pilots were patriots to a man and refused to guide the King's navy through the shoals. After the war, however, life became increasingly peaceful and prosperous, interrupted only by ferocious storms that inundated the banks and caused chaos in the exposed communities. *The Washington Gazette* reported that after a hurricane in August 1899: "the whole island is a complete wreck...the sea broke over Ocracoke in waves that were 20 and 30 feet high. Thirty-three homes were destroyed and two churches were wrecked. Practically every house was damaged. Mr. George Buckman, honored citizen of this town, and Henry Blango, a colored cook, were drowned... boats were sunk or were dashed to pieces against the shore. There was much suffering here."

The idea of any "suffering" in the Ocracoke of today seems most unlikely. This is a mellow little place (I've always wanted to use the word "mellifluous" in some context, and it's just about right here). White cottages slumber under the generous shade of live oaks, loblollies, and cedars; sandy paths meander through the "old village"; cozy hotels and inns promise simple comforts through the summer days and evenings; small restaurants are redolent with the aromas of she-crab soup, oyster stew, Ocracoke clam chowder, broiled fish from the charter boats, crabcakes, and big pink shrimp full of sea tang and that special sweetness only found in fresh seafood.

Summers can seem a little hectic here with a doubling and tripling of the town's 600 resident population. Because of relative ease of access, Ocracoke is becoming a popular vacation spot with adventurous travelers. Fishermen come here to charter boats and play Hemingway for a day in search of marlin, tuna, and bass (although most seem to end up with a more modest selection of mackerel, flounder, sea trout, and whiting). Bird-watchers lose themselves in the silent dunes and salt marshes north of the little town where you can wander for hours and never see another human. They might however be surprised by wild "banker" ponies, although their numbers are dwindling and

The Ocracoke Lighthouse

there's talk of moving them off Ocracoke altogether. No one is quite sure how the original ponies got here but tales of their being left by Sir Walter Raleigh, deposited by Cortez, or dumped by pirates, abound.

Families go clamming in the shallows off Teach's Hole (the site of Blackbeard's decapitation) or spend time at the visitors center and the demure white lighthouse which has now become a symbol of the community. Originally constructed in 1823, this plump, 75 foot tower is one of the oldest still in use on the Atlantic coast. Photograhers vie to capture the best composition of tower, white fence, and wind-shaped pines—all under a blue Ocracoke sky.

A short walk away, not far from the new school, is the British cemetery, a tiny appendage to a larger burial ground, occupied by four British sailors washed ashore on May 14, 1942, after the HMS Bedfordshire was sunk by one of the many German submarines operating off the coast during World War II.

History enthusiasts take charter boat trips across to the remnants of Portsmouth, barely visible across Ocracoke inlet. This was once the largest town on the Outer Banks and as equally renowned as Ocracoke for the quality and reliability of its pilots. Five hundred people once lived here; now much of the land is swamped at high tide and the last two permanent residents moved off-island in 1971. All that remains today are the prim Methodist chapel with its shingle-clad tower and immaculate white clapboard walls, a scattering of restored homes, a schoolhouse, and two cemeteries, set on slightly higher ground and edged by pines and myrtles.

Take time to explore Ocracoke's sandy lanes and chat with the locals, who seem to tolerate tourists with a kind of bemused indifference. Conversation can be difficult; like Tangier and Smith Islands, the dialect of the Ocracokers seems to possess the thick resonance of southern English counties, full of "ois" and long "aaahs" and a leisurely delivery that speaks of tranquil days around the circular harbor of Silver Lake. Shrimp and crab boats huddle here at the docks, safe from the fickle tides and sudden gales that have swept more than 500 vessels onto the reefs and beaches between Cape Henry and Cape Lookout in the last three centuries.

"Those toides don' aarf come in furious a'toimes. Oi've seen 'em switch so fast seems loike you've fallen 'sleep. It mommicked me a'first but oi felt more ca'm next in. Oi disremember when oi was laast caught short—long toime a'reckon." The old sailor was sitting on a wooden crate by one of the wharves overlooking the harbor. He'd come to fish but seemed to have changed his mind. "Sometoimes you think you'll fish a bit and then you don't. Makes no matter, which way it goes."

He had one of those leathery faces, deep brown with creases that buckled and rearranged themselves in new patterns every time he laughed. And he laughed a lot. He chuckled at the camera-happy tourists, at a frowning father desperately seeking respite from a gaggle of brawling offspring, at four seagulls fighting over a scrap of fish, at the idiosyncracies of his own life.

"Oi'd plans to be an engineer, took all the trainin' an thaat, then oi decided diff'rent and never left. Started shrimpin' and that was it with th' engineerin'."

Foy Shaw and Larry Williams at the Island Inn are more recent newcomers who share similar sentiments.

"You get hooked by the place," Larry told me as we sat sipping wine in the lounge of the Inn. "I know its tiny—tiny isn't the word—it's 'titchy'—but there's so much going on here it's like being in a big city. I came about seven years ago and plan on staying at least another seven—maybe seventy." Larry watches his customer's faces anxiously as they emerge after dinner.

"I'll cook anything, if I'm given enough time. Often they'll come in with fish they've caught and I'll do that for them—or chicken and shrimp Ariosto, that's one of my specialties, or my stewed shrimp and corn dumplings—that's a gem, and the she-crab soup. I season that—chef's secret—with marigold leaves and a bit of lemon and float a marigold flower head on top. People seem to love it."

Ocracoke attracts all kinds during the summer months, from frenzied workaholics in search of elusive peace, to reclusives coming to play hermit-beachcombers for a week or two out on the broad sands. In recent years things have become more commercial and hotel space has increased at an alarming rate. But the town still possesses a quaint integrity, with its low-profiled homes protected by live oaks and pines, remnants of private graveyards in the gardens, white fences along the paths, Jack Willis' and Corkey's stores on main street, and, as a constant reminder of island heritage, the altar in the Methodist chapel constructed from old ships' timbers.

"Oi don' know no better place n' this 'un," the fisherman by Silver Lake told me, "and if there 'appens t'be one, oi don' want to know."

Even Sir Walter Raleigh would have agreed. His colonists called the Outer Banks "The goodliest land under the cope of heav'n."

So who am I to argue?

One of Ocracoke's Lanes

16. Cape Lookout and The Core Banks

Back to Basics

There was something about the little brown leaflet that appealed to my pioneering instincts. It was entitled *"Camping on Cape Lookout National Seashore"* and warned of the primitive nature of this lonely 30 mile stretch of barrier island beach.

The terrain, it stated, "is generally sandy, roadless, with low dunes, and few trees. No stores or transportation are available... In the summer, when biting insects and heat are at their peak, find an area where winds blow across water or sands before reaching the campsite... protect yourself with a potent insect repellant... Weather conditions can change dramatically... squalls, commonly appearing as a line of dark clouds, can generate lots of rain, high winds and lightning... reduce your chances of being struck by getting as low as possible, digging into the sand if necessary...if you're notified of hurricanes return to the mainland as soon as possible... To withstand the strong winds a tent must be firmly anchored in the sand. In a pinch tie the guy wire to a piece of debris or equipment which has a large surface area and bury it in the sand. You must bring your own water. Emergency water can be found by digging one to three feet below the surface in the grassy sand flats behind the dunes."

Marvellous! An ideal place to play shipwrecked sailor for a day or a week; no people, no towns or stores—only the towering black and white 125 year old Cape Lookout lighthouse rising from the scrub at the southern end of the Core Banks. There are plans to improve access out here and even to increase the range of recreational options, but on my visit I had the whole beach, as far as I could see in both directions, all to myself.

I welcomed the silence, the isolation, and the constant change one senses out here in the cream, green, and blue infinities—the winds and the tides altering the shapes of dunes, pushing the beaches back, creating new marshes and submerging others, rolling the islands over on themselves. These barrier strips are alive, always on the move, ebbing and flowing like the tides themselves, but on a time-scale too broad for human appreciation.

On the ocean side, feathery tops of sea oats rise out of the low dunes above the cord grass and sharp-edged marram. The Shackleford Banks, close by across Barden Inlet, boast larger dunes and extensive maritime forests of live oak, cedar, loblolly pine, and hornbeam. Planners envisage it as a wilderness area with private vehicles prohibited. Out here on the Core Banks the vegetation is more modest—clumps of briers, palmetto, mulberry, and vines huddling in the lea of the dunes on the edge of the marshes.

The island was characterized by an absence of movement and life. There were few scurries or flurries in the dune grasses and even the normally voracious herring gulls seemed oddly lethargic in the heaviness of late summer. Breezes blew erratically, full of sticky moisture and the tang of salt.

A mile or two up the beach from the lighthouse I sprawled on the warm sand and let the day drift slowly on. The surf hissed, the dry grasses behind me rattled and rasped together like shrivelled widows at a wake. A hawk circled slowly, its shadow flicking over the sand and disappearing in the curves of the dunes. A steady chirruping from the marsh meant there was life in there somewhere, but on the beach, nothing moved except the sand-grains, ever easing inland.

Of course all this emptiness and silence is a relatively recent state of affairs. Back in the sailing days the Cape was labelled on early maps as "Promontorium Tremendum"—the "horrible headland"—of shallow shoals and treacherous currents. It became a nautical cemetery, "The Graveyard of the Atlantic," for scores of unfortunate ships and boats, including a number of Spanish treasure ships en route home after looting forays in the Americas.

Ben Salter, who spent much of his life on Portsmouth Island way at the northern tip of the Core Banks, recalls the *John I. Snow* which "came ashore off Portsmouth in 1907. Her cargo was wearing apparel, all kinds; silk dresses, ladies undergarments, men's pants, shirts and even shoes. Also a complete hotel they were carrying to be put up in New York."

His delightful book, *Portsmouth Island,* gives a personal view of life in that once-thriving community. "The first automobile I ever saw was on the *John I. Snow.* It was more like a buggy than a car. It had side lights and large wheels. It was sold to a Mr. Robinson. Folks on the island salvaged most of the cargo and had a 'vendre' (auction). My father bought the large white columns that were part of the hotel, to go on the front porch."

He remembers other wrecks. "*Vera Cruz* came ashore in May 1903 with four hundred twenty-one men, women and children aboard. She also had the prettiest sheep I have ever seen. The people on Portsmouth Island opened

Cape Lookout Light Station

their homes and took in the unfortunate people. This was a burden; they had to feed, clothe and find places for them to sleep until they could get help. Then *Melrose* came ashore in 1908. Her cargo was salt. Her crew were Portuguese. The poor people were pitiful. They looked about half starved and sick."

"Then there was the *"Messenger of Peace"* in 1922. She was boarded by whiskey government officials as she was loaded with whiskey. She was en route from the Bahama Islands to New York. The men on the island had all the whiskey they wanted to drink for quite a while. And one of the last was the *Midgett* in 1952. Her cargo was wheat and plenty of groceries, coffee by the cases. You can still see part of the wreckage on the beach at low tide."

Even this secluded wilderness though has problems. There are still scores of abandoned vehicles, ugly rusting hulks left by fishermen, many still around the lighthouse area. Excessive use of four wheel drive and other sand vehicles is threatening the fragile ecology of the banks. Controversy still swirls around ways to protect the Cape Lookout lighthouse from being destroyed as the underpinning of sand is eroded by the ocean.

Two local inhabitants who love this stretch of coast, ex-restaurateur Tony Seamon and writer Bob Simpson, feel dismayed at the procrastination and incompetence of government agencies. "I could tell you tales of stupidity and bloody-mindness that would curl your conscience,"Bob fumed and pointed to a thick wad of reports and newspaper clippings. "You got about three days?"

Tony recently appeared on a TV documentary investigating ways to safeguard the lighthouse, and he was adamant about its preservation: "This is a symbol for us—it's been a symbol for shippers for generations, keeping them off the shoals. It's a part or our heritage and I think it justifies any expense to save it."

"Mack" Riddel, superintendent of the National Seashore, shares many of their concerns and hopes the recent "General Management Plan" for the area will help solve some of the worst problems. So far he has managed to ensure effective restoration of old Portsmouth village, almost 60 miles north of the lighthouse, and to substantially increase annual funding for the park. His previous experience at Cape Hatteras as supervisor of the $4.2 million beach nourishment program has steeled him for the challenges ahead. "It's never easy—even with apparently isolated places like the banks. There's always conflict—different groups fighting to protect their own special interests—naturalists, fishermen, hunters, residents, day-trippers, loners—they all want different things. Problem is they all seem to want them in the same place and that can make things a bit hot around here at times. The wonderful thing, though, about this place is its uniqueness—this is one of the wildest and most remote places in the eastern USA. There's a primitive freedom and adventure out here—a sense of self-sufficiency and survival, especially if you get caught in one of those storms or run out of fresh water. It's just you and the elements then. You get a new respect for nature—and yourself, too, if you're careful!"

In the tingling silences of the sands all problems and conflicts seem rather insignificant. Out here you can lose yourself for a day, returning to the quiet places in your mind where the unity of tides, dunes, ocean, and sky are reminders of those slow, steady earth-rhythms so often forgotten in the scurry of everyday life.

Glimpses of eternal time; flickers of infinity.

17. Daufuskie

Scenes from Gullah-Land

It was dark when the ferry boat phut-phutted out of the elegant oval harbor at Harbor Town on Hilton Head Island. The air was clammy, full of early morning perfumes—magnolia, eucalyptus, pine, and a tang of ocean. Strips of mist wafted over the still water and the lights of the apartment towers and shoreside boutiques were soon left behind as we eased into blackness.

"Coffee?"

I was the only passenger that morning on the boat. Sylvia Wampler handed me a cup of strong brew; her husband, John, was in the wheelhouse peering through the mists.

"Should clear further out," Sylvia assured me.

I was en route to Daufuskie, perhaps the most mysterious of all Southern islands. People I'd talked to on Hilton Head seemed reluctant to tell me anything about the place. Maybe they didn't know much. The islanders, almost all black, and many of them descendants of the original slave families, tend to be an insular lot who prefer the basic comforts of their isolated world to the fripperies of affluent mainland life. "Jes b' careful whatcha say over there and don' point cameras at 'em," I was warned by one elderly man on the dock before we left. "They's sensitive jes' 'bout everything. Likely as not you won't understand a word they's said. They's got their own speakin' ways. Most caint make nothin' of it—it's all fast and funny-talk. They sees you comin' an they'll be speakin' Gullah right off."

I asked Sylvia about Gullah.

"It's their own language—sort of a pidgin dialect with bits of the African Benta language thrown in. They're about the last to speak it round here. You can hear it sometimes in Savannah but its dying out now except on the islands. It's got a lovely sing-song sound mixed with jive-talk rhythms and a bit of 'sass.' That's about the only way you can describe it, kinda 'happy-sassy'!"

The water slapped the side of the small boat. The mists were lifting and a lemon light flecked the ripples and reeds on either side of Cooper River, a placid stretch of water, about half a mile wide in places, separating the mainland from the islands. Time moved as slowly as the boat.

"That Haig's Point on 'Fuskie," Sylvia told me a while later. In the early glimmerings of dawn the place looked deserted, a tangled wilderness of ancient live oaks with scraggly beards of spanish moss, high ragged grass, and eucalyptus trees, dripping bark. A white heron stood skeleton-stiff in the shallows and two ospreys circled above a bulbous nest, wary of alien dawn sounds.

Just as the sun yolked up from behind the silhouetted trees, I spotted the Daufuskie dock. There were people up and about even at that hour. Half a dozen black men stood in front of four battered trucks of indeterminate age watching and laughing as the boat nudged against the new pier.

"You got plans or anything?" Sylvia asked me.

I shook my head. As usual I'd come to let things take their own course.

"Well unless you want to wear yourself out walkin', better see if Jake'll give you a ride round. Jake Washington. You can't miss him. He's up by that red truck. He takes charge of everything round here. You'll be okay with him. Tell him to take you to see Jim and Carol Alberto at the school first. You'll likely get some more coffee there!"

I thanked her.

"Enjoy yourself. Oh—and watch out for copperheads."

I wished she hadn't said that.

It felt lonely, walking up the long dock from the boat. It felt even lonelier when I heard the group by the trucks talking Gullah at express-train speed—a jumble of thick, rotund sounds that never seemed to let up. Jake had his head buried deep in the innards of a battered red truck with no door handles and no windows. I sat on a lopsided bench under a live oak and waited. The sun was already warm. The men passed an early morning beer among themselves and plunged back into Gullah, everyone talking at once.

"Yer wantin' a ride?" Jake had one of those active faces, a patchwork of fleeting expressions, a quick scowl followed by an almost-smile. I joined him in the truck and we set off into the island along a sandy track.

"We's goin' to my place first. Need some wire." I nodded. He seemed preoccupied, so I sat back as best I could on the ripped vinyl seat and watched the sage-green tendrils of spanish moss as they moved ever so slightly in fleeting breezes. Shacks with corrugated-iron roofs, some brightly painted and others abandoned, peeped out from the thick undergrowth. A cow, wandering dozily through ground mists, turned to watch Jake's truck and the plume of dust trailing behind. We passed the Mary Field school and the Union Baptist

A Saufuskie Road

Church, a plain white building with a stubby tower and pediment supported on thin pillars. The track divided and Jake spun off to the left into an open field littered with a dozen ancient automobiles in various stages of dismemberment. An old boat lay in the taller grass and bits of engines, gear boxes, and back axles were strewn around the path to the house like the aftermath of a vulture orgy.

"Y'had breakfast already?"

I'd forgotten about breakfast.

"Y'like crabs. Crabmeat?"

I'd never tried crabs for breakfast.

"Tell th'girl to do you some." He pointed at the house, a simple shack at the edge of the field near a vegetable patch and a battered chicken coop. "I'll be in."

Jake's house was hot. A young girl, very thin, with deep dark eyes, smiled shyly and showed me into a tiny living room. A burning wood stove and a waist-high pile of cut logs filled one corner; their weight bowed the uncarpeted floor and the heat made me wince. A radio and two television sets were on loud; someone was dancing behind a closed door. The girl hovered by the doorway, waiting.

"Jake told me I should ask you to cook some crabs or something," I said. She giggled, twisted a pigtail, and vanished.

The walls of the room were dotted with family photographs, gaudy paintings of Jesus complete with halo and tiny glass tears, prints of country scenes torn from magazines, and a yellowed clipping about Jake written by Alex Haley. The noise and the heat increased. A bedroom door opened and a young black man in shorts peered out at me, then shut it again. The Donahue show was in full chatter with Chicago matrons giving the country their views on homosexual marriages.

I could see Jake in the yard, tugging electric cord from the gutted remnants of a 1968 Chevrolet. I strolled into the next room, a small lounge filled with vinyl-covered furniture, a gleaming stereo set, and more family photographs in gilded frames. It had an unused look.

The giggling girl returned with a plate of steaming deviled crabs, bread, tomato ketchup, and tabasco sauce, and placed them all daintily at the head of the table in the living room.

"You want Coke? Coffee's out."

I thanked her, sat down, and forked a little of the crab from a red shell. The morning came alive in a burst of flavors—peppers, celery, apple, big chunks of

tender crab—all mixed in a mush of crushed crackers and sparked by some palate-popping spices. I was on fire but the taste was too good to stop. Sweat tumbled down my cheeks, the stove burned even more brightly, and the girl watched me from the doorway as I melted away.

Daufuskie is known for the excellence of its deviled crabs and I had discovered the source. The island's oysters also once enjoyed a fine reputation around Savannah until recent pollution in the creeks and bays killed off the industry and all the jobs.

"More'n half of us were in oysters back in th' late fifties," Jake told me as we left the house, this time in a blue truck with windshield and door handles. " 'Fore that it was loggin'. We had a railroad then. 'Fore that it was boat-buildin' and farmin'. More than 1000 people lived here. 'Fore that it was plantation cotton but the weevil killed that off. Now th'aint nothin' much of nothin'."

The island, originally granted to a British naval captain, John Mungin, by George III in 1740, became a prosperous plantation after Independence under a Mr. Stoddard, who married one of Mungin's daughters. His Melrose estate was described by an enthusiastic visitor in 1862 as:

> *"the finest ever I have seen on this shore, an elegant and tasteful mansion, furnished with marble fireplaces and mantles and with an abundance of outbuildings. And such a garden there never was, I do believe. Stoddard kept an English gardener, whose residence was such that a prince might envy...Such walks, hedges, arbors, vines, graveled paths, shade trees, flowers of every hue, I never imagined. The grounds are all laid out on a very extensive scale, winding walks going in all directions, divided off by neatly trimmed hawthorn hedges; orange, lemon, fig, plum, cherry and peach trees in profusion. Amid the blossoming stocks stands the crown-lily of the island; a summer house of octagonal form, about ten feet across, surmounted by a cupola and a weather cock, with stained glass over the swinging glass windows and an arched roof. It is said there are 6,000 pieces of wood in this little house alone."*

Nothing remains of this palatial paradise except a few foundation stones but there's plenty of talk nowadays of new development. The northern part of the island has been purchased for large private estates and elite condominiums. Potential buyers are chauffered around the sandy tracks in a horse and buggy. Islanders are split about the idea of development but Jake has made up his mind.

"We stand to do good outa this. There'll be work buildin' and keepin' things runnin' smooth plus they're payin' good money for land—real good money—so it'll be six-pack days every day. No more ham bones and hash."

Politicking and pressure-group tactics still must run their course before final decisions are made but the heat is on and the 100 or so inhabitants of the island can sense change coming.

"Things need changin' on 'Fuskie." Then Jake banged the steering wheel and laughed. "Tha's where we usta live."

He stopped by an open field of high grass near the site of the Stoddard mansion and pointed to a series of gray stumps. "Tabby-shacks. Slave cabins. From when all this was cotton plantations."

I could see bits of eroded walls built from that durable combination of oystershells, lime, sand, and water.

"Th' Indians left us their garbage—piles of these shells—so we used 'em real good. So long you got a good roof these walls'd last long as bricks. Way back they got messed up bad by th' hurricane. Killed off most of the people 'cept those that could climb trees. That was round th' beginning this century; since then it's been all downhill for 'Fuskie."

We drove on to Haig's Point at the top of the island where a Victorian mansion with an elegant lighthouse tower peered over the reeds at Hilton Head Island. Nearby was the shed where the developers kept their buggy for transporting wealthy clients around future home-sites. Jake scowled and pointed at a four-foot high painted figurine of a coachman in hat and livery holding the hitching ring for the buggy-horse. He had a black painted face and piccaninny smile. I wondered how many islanders had been to see this little offensive statue.

We took a different track back down the island, winding around the roots of the live oaks, watching for deer. A snake whiplashed across the sandy dust. Jake aimed the truck at it and missed.

"Copperhead. There'll be another near."

We stopped by a worn brick structure with a thin roof. Two clapboard doors

Tabby remains
of old slave shacks
on Daufuskie

were opened and I could see cobwebbed shelves and alcoves inside. A sign over the lintel read "Silver Dew Winery."

"That was one of the Burn businesses. Arthur "Pappy" Burn started it up round 'bout 1953 and made pretty good fruit wines—huckleberry, dewberry, scuppernong—you name it. Didn't last long though. He packed up around 1956."

Members of the Burn family have been on the island for as long as most people can remember. Arthur Ashley Burn bought the old lighthouse at Bloody Point in 1925 and his son Alfred Lance brings the mail every day by boat from Savannah to the post office where his wife Billie is postmaster, notary public, and registrar.

We rode out of the shaded lanes to the beach. At nearby Bloody Point, according to island legend, a raiding party of Yemassee Indians who had attacked settlers, was cornered and slaughtered here in 1715. One escaped and swam to nearby Tybee. The blood of the others turned the beach red. Today it's very white against the green marsh grass and the dark line of pines and oaks. And quiet. Few visitors come here and island children fear the ocean almost as much as the mysterious "root doctors" whose cures and curses are still a discernible part of island tradition. The remnants of old tree stumps and gnarled roots in the sand give the place an eerie feel.

We drove back from the beach past the Silver Dew winery to the Mary Dunn cemetery, hidden in a grove of tangled trees at the end of a dark lane.

I stepped carefully between the old headstones and the ivy-shrouded brick vault with no name on it. There were fresh flowers on two of the graves. The ceramic jug at the head of Mary Martinangle's stone, dated April 2, 1790, was empty. More tassled beards of spanish moss drooped and swayed. Flies buzzed erratically in the thickening heat and my stomach still simmered from the deviled crab breakfast.

Jake and I parted company at the Mary Field School after I paid him for his services as guide. There was a glimmer of amusement in his eyes with overtones of something much deeper, an island knowingness that made me wonder what I could have asked him but didn't. He had told me briefly of his life as fisherman, farmer, mechanic, property-owner, clammer, snake-hunter, school janitor, and all-round entrepreneur. He had told me of island traditions, now dwindling or gone: The old Saturday night music parties, the "leg sessions" (which sounded more like excuses for brief bouts of wife-swapping), the fiery all-night church meetings, the feuds and family murders, the intricacies of the Gullah language, the overtones of voodoo in island customs,

A quiet creek on Haufuskie

the ghostly tales of Haig's Point, and the sidewheel steamers that once came from Savannah for Saturday night shindigs and left on Sunday morning with the occasional dead bodies of errant "outsiders." He told me all this in his low-key drawl that, frustratingly, kept lapsing into Gullah. But I knew there was more—much more.

Jim and Carol Alberto, the two teachers at the school, confirmed my feelings.

"We've been here for eight years and in some ways we know less about these people now. They're a strange lot—they keep so much inside. Even if they like you they're careful about what they say—how much they tell you. One guy has really got it in for us—he's determined to get us off the island. One year they had five teachers come and go! The guy I replaced stayed here three days. He had a teaching aide—a black—and he invited her over for dinner and the boyfriend heard, got mad as hell, and told him to his face he was going to kill him. That's one of the popular expressions here—'You gonna get murdered.' "

"Jake told you about the Saturday night bodies in the old steamer days? It's true. It was a deadly place in those days—about 30 years ago. Things are quieter now, but you still get the occasional gun shots in someone's door—look for the bits of rags stuck in the bullet holes to keep the flies out."

The Albertos live in a trailer at the side of the small white school-house, a young, healthy couple in their early thirties, still excited about life on the island.

"It really is a lovely place. We've got our own boat so if things get a bit hairy, which they can do, especially with this new black evangelist guy around—he really scares people—we just take off for one of the islands or Savannah and get away from it all for a while. But we always want to come back. We love the kids. God knows what'll happen to most of them, though. We try to get them ready to deal with the world off-island—when they go to high school on Hilton. But it's hard. They get dumped on, they get pregnant, they get in all kinds of trouble over there. It's too much of a shift for most of them."

"Pat Conroy tried to help make some changes but that only got him fired. Y'remember Pat Conroy? He wrote *The Water is Wide*—they made a film about him with Jon Voigt - *Conrack*. He really showed the school board what a mess they were making of their job and that got him fired for 'insubordination.' You wouldn't believe what things were like out here when he first came! He took over a class of 18 children and not one knew the alphabet; fifteen were below first-grade reading level; most of them thought Daufuskie was one of the nine planets and that Savannah was the largest city in the world! Things are better now but we still have a heck of a lot more to do if these kids are ever going to get half a chance in the real world.''

The two classrooms in the tiny school were brightly colored and full of ''visual stimulants''—charts, suspended mobiles, maps, model planes and boats, prints, photos, fish in tanks, paintings. The kids even put out their own magazine of poetry, drawings, bits of island history and comments on island life:

> I like Daufuskie because it doesn't have many cars
> and not any police. It is very quiet over here. I
> like to run around and play. I wish we had an ice
> cream parlor, a gym, and a playground. I wish we
> had a museum and we could put arrowheads and pottery
> in it.
>
> Larry Forrest
>
> If I was the sky I'd make the clouds pink and yellow
> I'd make rainbows reach across the world.
> I'd make people fly without air planes
> and I'd let people sit on the clouds.
>
> Michelle Smith.

I had the afternoon to myself and set off on a slow ramble along sandy tracks. The air was butter-thick under the oaks. Except for the occasional battered truck and its spume of white dust, the island was silent under a moist Southern sun. Only a few years back people moved around in ox-carts. Today, everyone seemed to be indoors. There's virtually no work on the island now, so life has taken on the lazy rhythms of a leisured population. Even the dogs seemed half-hearted in their barks and snarls as I wandered past the tin-roofed shacks set back from the soft sand paths. Patches of swamp glistened in the half-light of the forest. They say there are alligators and hundreds of deadly snakes but I didn't see any. Occasional breaks in the thick underbrush of thatch palm and palmetto offered vistas across reeds out to the mainland. A tiny boat drifted by. A fishing rod dangled from the bow and a pair of bare feet peeped up over the side; someone was snoozing the afternoon away dreaming of catfish for supper. I sat in the shade under one of the oaks and sketched. No one disturbed me and for a while Daufuskie was all mine.

A couple of hours later, after an erratic exploration of meandering paths, I arrived back at the island cooperative store by the ferry dock. A number of elderly residents were sitting on the bench by the screened-in pavilion where they served deviled crabs and other island specialities to groups of summer tourists. Inside the store, a large bright building, the shelves are stocked with a limited array of offerings: flour, crackers, ketchup, mayonnaise, various hot sauces, and an aisle of aluminium pans big enough to bathe babies. The young man at the checkout counter looked like he hadn't seen a customer all day and seemed concerned that I might disturb his peace. The wall behind his head was covered with small colored photographs of island residents and a few fine black and white prints by Jeanne Moutoussamy-Ashe, wife of the tennis player Arthur Ashe, whose book of photographs on Daufuskie had been recently published.

A crowd began to collect outside on the track down to the dock, slowly at first, then as it got closer to the 5:30 p.m. arrival time of the ferry, the numbers increased. The old men sat silently together on the oyster shell river bank sharing beers; a group of younger men huddled among the roots of a live oak passing a bottle in a paper bag, and five young girls, frisky and giggling, were lost in their own little world of whispers and furtive glances.

Then, as if by pre-arranged signal, the ferry boat eased around the wooded shoulder of the island and Jake Washington rolled up in a green truck this time, ready to supervise the unloading. His wife and two of his daughters had been to Hilton Head shopping and he was the first down at the boat, heaving bags and sacks up the long walkway. The rest of the onlookers followed, helping with the haulage, making wisecracks, slapping shoulders. For a few minutes the dock was full of noise and laughter. I waited until all the lugging was over and then rejoined Sylvia and John Wampler by the wheelhouse as the boat turned in a broad arc of brown ripples and headed for Harbor Town. I looked back at the dock and it was silent again. The trucks had gone, the people had gone, back down the tracks to their homes under the oaks. The lights were out in the store. Daufuskie was closed up and the only stranger that day was gone, on his way back to a more familiar world up the Cooper River.

Pat Conroy was right. The water is wide when you make the journey to this strange island only 18 miles from Savannah City Hall. And that's just the way Daufuskie people like it.

18. Sapelo

A True "Place Apart"

Even the name is gentle, evoking images of slow Southern afternoons in the shade under live oaks; afternoons stirred by breezes and a hammock hardly moving; afternoons in a wooden boat out in reedy lagoons catching crabs for supper. And the island, one of the Golden Isles of Georgia (also known as the Sea Islands, and named the Guale islands by Pedro Menendez in 1606) lives up to such expectations. This is a quiet, unspoiled backwater, a true "place apart," where little is likely to change as long as it remains protected by two wildlife refuges, a fully-equipped marine institute, and an estuarine sanctuary at the southern end of the island.

The ferry was late leaving the dock at Meridian, a small waterside village littered with shrimp boats. Five portly blacks stood by the dock ready with fishing poles and wide nets, talking non-stop in Gullah, the same strange dialect I'd heard on Daufuskie. I seemed to be the only passenger intent on exploring the island; the others were residents or members of Georgia University's Marine Institute (bearded, professional, and serious). A young girl arrived, pretty Penny Haythorn, who introduced herself as my personal guide and began a lengthy description of island character, all in a sleepy Southern drawl.

The boat eased down the river, slicing through mirrored images of reeds, woods, and high thunderhead clouds. I could see thick clumps of oysters on the river banks, thousands of gnarled gray shells huddled together in some strange kind of amorphous dependency. Seagulls, seeking snacks in the froth, skimmed low over the boat's wake. Penny flung a handful of biscuit crumbs overboard and turned twenty birds into a whirling frenzy of wings and snapping beaks.

"Something about gulls I don't like. They're really vicious creatures, y'know." She managed to looked both disgusted and amused at the display of raw aggression. The blacks stood with their fishing poles, watching, while the rest of the professional passengers sat in the cabin, eyes glazed in the sticky morning heat.

After a half hour or so, we docked among more shrimp boats on Sapelo

One of Sapelo's magnificent live oaks

island. Green-gray swathes of reeds stretched away to the north; a low purple line of live oaks marked the higher dry ground. Penny immediately started arguing with two men in jeans and baseball caps about available transport. Normally, an old bus is used to take visitors on an island tour but there was no bus today and it would have been a little oversized for two travelers anyway. Finally she convinced them they could do without a rather ramshackle jeep and we climbed in, only to find the reverse gear inoperable. The men chortled in the shadows of their caps and Penny was furious.

"Stop foolin' around and push this lousy machine so we can git movin'."
This Southern girl had fire too!

Curiously, they obeyed and we were off like jackrabbits, dust flailing behind us, bright blue skies above. "Who the heck needs reverse anyway. We'll do jes' fine," said Penny.

There are no paved roads on the island so we sort of slid-skidded along sometimes red, sometimes white sandy tracks between oaks wrapped in tendrils of vines. Much of the low brush seemed to have been cleared; there were occasional clusters of palmetto but mostly it was high summer-bleached grass stretching out to the reeds. The air was very still, the only movement coming from the jeep as we bumped along the western edge of the island.

Remnants of "tabby-shacks" hunched in the high grass by the side of the track, wind-worn stumps of walls made of oyster shells, lime, and sand. These were once Spanish mission buildings and later used as slave houses when the island thrived as a prosperous plantation and center for innovative agricultural experiments in the early 1800s. One of the most optimistic (if somewhat eccentric) settlers here was the Marquis de Montalet, whose faded estate we found nearby at the end of an avenue of dying pecan trees. The barn has been preserved but the old mansion with its tall chimneys crumbled in the scrub near smaller tabby-built structures.

"He was a real sweetie," Penny gushed. "He came with a black chef, Cupidon, who everybody thought was the most valuable asset on the island. The Marquis had been a planter down in Santa Domingo before coming up this way to Georgia. He'd heard there were some French property owners anxious to sell their estates. When he came to visit Sapelo in 1801, he found Monsieur and Madame de Boisfeuillet living here in something like luxury on their "Bourbon" estate, so he decided to settle just up the road in a house he called Le Chatelet—the slaves called it "Chocolate."

I tried to imagine what the place must have felt like in the early 1800s with its avenue of trees, views over the reeds and lagoons, and gourmet dinners prepared by the famous Cupidon. Apparently the Marquis was a fanatical truffle-lover and insisted that, with all the live oaks around, Sapelo must be a haven for that exquisite fungus normally found among the roots of oak trees. So he brought in Alphonse, a highly trained truffle-hunting pig, and spent hours every week tugging the frustrated creature around on a leash, pushing his sensitive snout into every root system he could find. After years of Alphonse's abortive sniffing and snorting the Marquis wrote forlornly: "I thought we might one day find them. I would truly that we might, for the eating of truffles makes men more gay and women more tender—and in this country we indeed need them. Mon Dieu!"

The Marquis was only one of Sapelo's notable landowners. A Scotsman, Thomas Spalding, heir to the Barony of Ashantilly, managed to buy up much of the island in the early 1800s from nervous French landlords who were reluctant to return to revolution in their homeland and who, because of the loss of their French estates, needed funds urgently. With Carnegie-like dedication, Spalding created a flourishing plantation by introducing Sea Island cotton, operating a sugar mill, raising full-blooded Aberdeen Angus bulls, and selling cut oak for shipbuilding. He also supervised the tabby-based construction of "South End Place," a magnificent columned palace at the southern end of the island where he and his family lived in "princely pomp" (according to one impressed visitor) until the onset of the Civil War. In spite of a Spalding family tradition of protest against slaves and slavery, Thomas saw no alternative to black labor in Georgia but salved his conscience somewhat by vowing that: "They shall be more serfs than slaves on my land. I shall civilize them, and better their condition."

And from all accounts he was true to his word, keeping work loads light and refusing to sell any of his workers during his lifetime. Before the eventual collapse of his estate during the Civil War, Spalding claimed that "this plantation is the happiest form of peasant life the world can show." Obviously the world was not convinced.

We moved off again down the long avenue of trees and turned north along more meandering sandy tracks. Twice we got stuck in soft patches, which brought forth remarkably colorful epithets from Penny about non-existent reverse gears and the incompetence of island mechanics.

She seemed pre-occupied though as we drove, her supply of Marquis and Cupidon stories having run dry. Then she yelped and brought the jeep to a halt in a gloomy section of oak forest, dark even at mid-morning. "Thought I'd missed it. I love this place—come and see it." I noticed the back wheels had again ended up in loose sand. "Oh never mind—you can push it out when we get back."

Penny scampered off through the high grass heading for an odd earth mound near the edge of the reeds. "C'mon, just come and look at this place." I climbed up a steep bank and found myself peering down into a round enclosure about 80 feet across and 20 feet high, rather like one of those defensive circles so loved by the Picts and other warring tribes in England back in prehistoric times. Only this was different, very different. The whole circle consisted of millions, maybe billions, of packed oyster shells covered by a thin layer of earth, grass, and a few stunted trees.

"Indians!"

Penny did a little pirouette in the center of the earth-ring (my guide was turning out to be all show-biz) and continued a little breathlessly: "This is where he sat, right here, the chief of the Creek Indians, about 4,000 years ago. He was fat—really gross y'know—and spent most of his time just sitting right here, eating tons of oysters and throwing shells over his shoulder to make the circle."

I knew shell rings were once a familiar sight on the offshore islands of Georgia and South Carolina but never expected to find such a perfect example, spoiled only by openings obviously hacked through by insensitive contemporaries. Penny was dancing again. "Can't you just see them all here. Scores of them sitting around munching through all those oysters and watching their ring get higher and higher, all more than 4,000 years ago!"

Her enthusiasm was contagious; I've certainly heard of far less pleasant ways of passing a lifetime and there was a part of me that envied the fat Indian chief and his gluttonous cronies.

As I'd feared, the jeep was stuck and it was my job to push it out while Penny spun the wheels with fury, covering me in white dust.

"This thing is supposed to have four wheel drive," I reminded her.

"Oh really. Where is it?"

"Push that lever next to the gearstick and see if that helps." She did, and it did. The jeep sprang forward like a kangaroo on a fast roll and left me chest down in the sand with a mouthful of grit. Out of a cloud came a happy voice.

"Hey—great. It worked!"

I think at that point I decided that if I ever wrote anything at all about this lovely island, Penny would have to feature prominently as part of the experience.

We drove on to where the trail ended rather abruptly at the edge of a swamp.

The Indian Mound · Sapelo

"That's all marsh through there." Penny pointed at a tangle of oaks and palmetto. "Then on the other side you've got Blackbeard Island, the national wildlife refuge. On the maps they show Sapelo as one island, but actually it's two big ones and a couple of tiny ones all separated by marshes."

I asked if the island was yet one more of the east coast's Blackbeard head-quarters.

"Not only that. They also keep getting all excited about hidden treasure over there. He's supposed to have lived in the old mission for a while sometime in the early 1700s and buried Spanish treasure on the island in a place called Money-Old-Fields. They say it's guarded by this terrible headless ghost all dolled up with pistols, cutlasses, and daggers! It's pretty wild over there—high dunes and some really scary hollows, all swampy. Not many visitors see it. They've got a lot of wild turkeys—they must be one of the brightest birds around y'know, and they've got chachalaca—Mexican pheasants—and some white tailed deer, big sea turtles, and possums, hundreds of possums, and racoons, too, though they're dying out so they say—and snakes. They get garter snakes, green snakes, scarlet-kings, black racers, cottonmouths, water moccasins, corn snakes—and salamanders. I've seen most of them."

Penny paused for breath and pointed out into the marshy lagoon at the edge of the track. "See—there. Near that log. There's one. A water moccasin." We watched as the little black head moved rapidly across the water in a flurry of ripples. "He's movin' fast. Likely there's an alligator on his tail." I must have looked startled. We were standing quite a distance from the safety of the jeep and I had no inclination to dally with alligators.

"Heck you're standin' right on his slide anyway." She pointed at muddy skid marks leading down to the water on either side of the track.

"This water on the south side is mainly spring fed, so, no salt. On the other side you've got brackish water, tidal, plenty of salt. They like to switch once in a while and they do it right here at the narrowest part of the track. That's what those slides are. Look at the claw marks and look there where the grass is all pushed down, the mud's still wet. Must have been one by jes' recent."

I was back in the jeep fast. Penny ambled along, smiling. "Heck, c'mon, they're not so tough as they look y'know. They keep their distance worse'n you do."

All I could think of was a noncommital "uh-huh."

We returned by another route through the interior where the live oaks seemed much more dense and ominous than along the edge of the island.

"They have a saying about them." Penny was playing guide again. "They say a live oak takes a hundred years to grow, lives for another hundred, and then takes another hundred to die. Funny thing is they look the same all along; even a baby live oak looks ancient."

I paused to sketch one particularly enormous specimen with a branch-span of over 80 feet, a contorted explosion of tentacle-like appendages, thick barked, moss-covered, and bearded with the now familiar tendrils of spanish moss. Bits of broken and discarded branches lay all around in the high grass; tiny ferns and a few dwarf palmetto grew in the forks above our heads, a score of birds twitted and chirped in the highest branches. The tree seemed benevolent in its old age, a nurturing place for all the life of the forest.

And then came Hog Hammock, a collection of simple clapboard shacks scattered around a labyrinth of tracks and paths, shaded by more enormous oaks and home of the island's small black population. Like the residents of Daufuskie Island in South Carolina, the occupants of Hog Hammock prefer to keep to themselves and don't particularly welcome "snoopers" and "'fessors." Their lives seem little changed since the early 19th century; they fish when they feel like it, cultivate small kitchen gardens, collect around Benny's store for slow afternoon debates, and still believe in folk medicine and "the old ways". Most of the children now go by boat to school in Darien on the mainland and the old blue school building in the Hammock has become a community center. The place has a docile feel; nothing much happens here and nobody much cares. Penny was nervous of my taking photographs. "They're not too keen on that y'know—and anyway we shouldn't really be here. Let's go."

We almost hit the soft sand again but this time the four wheel drive helped us through and we emerged on the "autobahn," a broad, arrow-straight earth road built through the forest by German engineers during one of the island's "improvement phases." For a mile or two we felt separated from the island on this 120 foot wide thoroughfare.

Then suddenly we arrived at South End Place, the old home of Thomas Spalding, resurrected and refurbished by his successor, Howard Coffin, automobile pioneer of Hudson Motors fame. Like Spalding, Coffin was a man of visions and ambitious schemes and he set about recreating a flourishing island economy by founding an oyster and shrimp packing industry, replanting Sea Island cotton, laying out pine forests, building roads, installing electricity, and raising cattle. As part of his master plan he restored South End Place as a sumptuous stucco mansion complete with reflecting pools and

Sapelo's South End
Place

statuary, an elaborately muralled indoor swimming pool, an enormous ballroom, a basement bowling alley, exotic bedrooms, and a bar with a ship-like interior. He even renamed the island Sapeloe, restocked its ponds and forests with a wide variety of game and fish, and invited the rich and famous to enjoy his boats, his house, and his gracious Southern hospitality.

"I always get goosebumps when I come here," Penny said, gazing at the splendid Italianate house from the statue-adorned reflecting pool. Landscaped grounds stretched away in all directions with billiard table lawns, ponds, and dainty footbridges. "Just think of all the people—all those Presidents and whatnot who've walked around this pool—Herbert Hoover, Calvin Coolidge—they say Charles Lindbergh came here—and Jimmy Carter. He came quite often when he was governor of Georgia. He really loved it."

After Coffin's death the estate was purchased by Richard J. Reynolds, the tobacco-king, who reinforced all his predecessors' efforts and added a sprawling dairy complex and elite resort accommodations, later a camp for young school boys, and a marine institute for the University of Georgia. Further land purchases by the state from the Reynolds family enabled the creation of the wildlife refuge in the northern part of the island and the estuarine sanctuary in the southern sector around South End Place.

We ended our all-too-brief exploration of Sapelo on the dunes overlooking Nanny Goat Beach, a short drive from the mansion. The sea was choppy, the breeze warm and strong, and the broad beach empty. For a while I had the whole airy place to myself; great thunderheads still grew white and bulbous high over my head, and the silence of the place numbed my mind for a few wonderful moments.

Then came Penny:

"This stupid jeep's gone and got stuck again... ."

19. Lignumvitae

An Island Forgotten by Time

Pelicans clustered around the boat dock by a store, all worn woodslats and deep slabs of shade. A sun-bleached sign on poles towered above the palm trees offering boat rentals to Lignumvitae. Apparently this was the only way to get out to the small mysterious island and no one seemed in any hurry to take me there. A stout middle-aged man with a stubbly grey beard sprawled in an old armchair sipping beer. A woman, thin and fluttery, hopped about inside the store straightening pamphlets, brushing the counter, and whispering to herself. The man scattered a handful of nuts across the planks while three brown pelicans with black eyes and tiny hooks at the end of their beaks, waddled forward like elderly pensioners to snap up the treats. The man laughed, I smiled, and the pelicans made odd clacking sounds with their leathery pouches.

It was 8:15 a.m. and hot. As I was the only passenger around, the cost of a two-way three-mile boat trip was negotiated to my disadvantage.

"Sure you can't russle up four or five more?" the man asked. A spring poked out from the torn vinyl seat. "Make it a lot cheaper for you."

"Wish I could."

"Well—give it ten minutes or so, maybe you'll be lucky."

I wasn't. At 8:45 a.m. the man raised himself slowly, crushed his beer can and wandered down the dock to start the engine. The woman peered anxiously at us from the dark interior of the store. I grinned and she disappeared.

We moved off in a great arc across the purple-blue water avoiding coral shoals just below the surface and dangerous sandy shallows. To the south of the road bridge, which carries The Overseas Highway (Route 1) down to the "Conch Republic" of Key West, I could see parts of infamous Indian Key. This once-prosperous "wrecking station" was made the county seat of Dade County in 1836 and owner Jacob Housman built himself a mini-kingdom here complete with landscaped gardens, cisterns, paved streets, a Masonic lodge, and an appropriately palatial mansion for himself.

All went well until the wrecking and indian trade soured and Housman was obliged to mortgage the property. The arrival of a Dr. Henry Perrine and his

The Garden · Lignumvitae

family in 1878 saw the island transformed into a botanical laboratory under the protection of government forces. Unfortunately, due to some military snafu, these forces were absent on the day when a hundred Seminole Indians raided the Key in 1840 and massacred Dr. Perrine and some of his assistants. They had really hoped to capture Houseman who had turned against his Indian traders and was offering their scalps at $200 each to the government. Housman died an ugly death, however, a year after the raid, crushed by a reefed ship he was trying to salvage. Since then, the old warehouses and homes have crumbled into the palmetto and thatch palms and only the occasional curious visitor breaks the uneasy silence here.

It's hard to imagine furious storms, wrecked ships, and bloodlusting indians on a blue-balmy day in the Keys. Lignumvitae offers a more appropriately tranquil history of virtually undisturbed evolution. As we neared the island the thick fringes of mangroves and dwarf palms opened to reveal a stately white mansion set back on a lawn of velvety grass.

"That's the only house on the island. The rest is just as God made it."

It was difficult to hear my personal boatman over the growling of the outboard engine and even more difficult to pay attention as we nudged up against the narrow wharf. A haze of fat black mosquitoes descended on my exposed limbs with an avaricious glee bordering on the obscene.

"Y'should have sprayed," my boatman told me. There were no mosquitoes around him, I noticed. "'Quitos here are real vicious—killers." He knew I'd forgotten my spray and that only seemed to increase his amusement. The more I slapped and wafted and cursed, the more aggressive they became. "Better run like hell for the house. There's a guide up there to take you around. See if you can get some of her spray."

Torn between a desire to ask why he hadn't mentioned these man-eaters before we'd left his boat dock and a need to seek a safe haven as quickly as possible, I chose self-preservation and scampered through the tiny gate, past cast-iron cannons set in the lawn, and up the steps of the big house. The State Park guide who had seen my plight stood with the door already open behind the screen and showed sympathy by spraying my fiery limbs.

"It's not 100% guaranteed, but it does for most people." She gave me a visual workover. "In your case you may have problems—they seem to go for light-skinned, red-haired types, particularly if they've got a bit of flesh on their bones."

The day wasn't quite working out the way I'd planned. By 9 a.m. I'd paid a ransom for my transport, been left defenseless against the ravages of a thousand probosci, and been informed that I was an overweight, mosquito-prone, redhead.

Fortunately the spray helped and as we left the cool confines of the house, with its small museum of turn-of-the-century artifacts, I could finally turn my attention to this lovely unspoiled place, one of the last undeveloped keys in the Florida chain.

My guide, Mary, was a kaleidescope of information, painting word pictures of early island owners who seemed to share a common goal of botanical preservation. The 1919 Matheson family house has been maintained in near-authentic condition, although much of it had to be rebuilt following the 1935 hurricane which brought the lowest pressure ever recorded in the western world and a tide height increase of twenty feet. Smaller keys were totally submerged; structures on Indian Key were flattened; Flagler's famous railroad to Key West was wiped out and never rebuilt, and half the population of the Keys disappeared forever into the maelstrom. Much of Lignumvitae was swamped (even though a 16½ foot high point makes it the Matterhorn of the Florida Keys) and the Matheson house lost its roof and some walls. A tiny reinforced concrete structure at the rear of the house, with a four inch thick door and the impregnability of an air-raid shelter, was built as protection against similar disasters.

Mary took me down the shady paths, pointing out strange trees in the tropical gloom: Jamaican dogwood, strangler figs, poisonwood, gumbo limbo, pigeon plum, ironwood, mastic and the writhing Lignum Vitae itself—the "Tree of Life."

These eerie, ancient creatures are now almost unique to the island and many are well over 1,000 years old. Back in the days of sailing ships they were valued for their rock-like density (Lignum Vitae is one of the few woods that sinks), their immunity to termites and shipworms, and their oily self-lubricating quality which make them ideal for pulleys and bearings. Even the medicinal resin, particularly useful for rheumatic ailments, was valued. Inevitably the once abundant groves in lower Florida were quickly used up by the Spanish Conquistadores and later by the British Navy. Now the species is almost extinct in North America and Lignumvitae Key is their last sizeable stronghold. They lurk warily in the shadows, their roots exposed in the shallow top soil, their branches curling like boa constrictors. One particularly venerable specimen, hardly eight feet high and said to be over 1,500 years old, leaned precariously over a murky sink hole, its branches reaching out for air and light to maintain its imperceptible growth.

An ancient Lignum Vitae
—Boa constrictor forms
in the gloom

We seemed to walk for miles through the green half-light, following the remains of a coral-stone wall more than 3,000 feet long, which divides the key in two. It is said to be the work of early Spanish settlers who wished to segregate themselves from their Indian slaves. Mary talked of the old Indian burial grounds, the remains of an old Spanish settlement, and the dangers of touching the resin of the aptly-named poisonwood tree (worse than poison ivy). We saw strangler figs with aerial roots and watched two golden orb weavers spin three-dimensional webs from the strongest of silver threads, capable of capturing small birds. We almost had a dispute with an enormous horned "crab" spider (its body bears an uncanny resemblance to a miniature crab), whose bites can be painful. Florida tree snails with rainbowed shells moved slowly up the bark of nearby poisonwood trees.

"This is pretty much the way the Conquistadores must have seen it," Mary told me, as we avoided yet one more enormous spider's web across the trail. "We've tried to understand and keep natural ecological systems intact. We introduced a few new species like the Key Largo wood rat—the creature was almost extinct so we had to give it a home somewhere—and we brought in a small herd of Virginia white-tail deer and some racoons. Otherwise all the things you see here have been around for a few thousand years."

We paused to peer into a wooded hollow, damp and musky. "She's in there!" Mary grabbed my arm and pointed to a shadowy bundle of twigs. A tiny rodent face with big whiskers and wise, sleepy eyes peeped out at us. "She's my favorite—one of the wood rats—I watched her build her nest last year and we've become close friends. She usually sleeps about this time, when it starts to get hot. She has at least three other nests she uses but this seems to be her favorite."

Mary pointed to a large bundle of twigs and dried thatch palm leaves on the other side of the trail. "That's one of hers too. See that path?" She pointed to a narrow stretch of earth, free of vegetation. "They clear routes like that between nests so they can see any dangers—racoons, rat snakes, things like that. They don't like taking chances in the scrub."

A huge gray moth, with a wingspan well over five inches, fluttered past my face as we stood on the coral edge of the key looking out across a lagoon through tangles of mangroves, their exposed roots arching out of the ocean. "They only absorb fresh water even though they're growing in sea-water. The turbo-pressure in their roots is incredible—almost 900 pounds per cubic inch. A kind of reverse osmosis takes place and the plant literally sucks out non-saline water and discards the rest."

Above our heads air-plant orchids flourished in the crooks of mahagony branches. Earth-colored lizards flicked across the coral in lightening darts, hardly visible in the sparse sunlight filtering through the canopy of treetops. From the rotting corpses of dead trees appeared new trees, reflecting the standard life cycle of a tropical hardwood hammock. Everywhere there was growth—from the infinitely slow nurturing of the Lignum Vitae tree, to the fleeting light-winged insects sparkling for a few hours of life in shafts of sunlight.

We returned to the open lawns of the house, guarded by the cannons from the British warship HMS *Winchester*, which sank nearby in 1965. My mosquito spray had lost its effectiveness and as we emerged from the forest they descended again with pent-up fury. After hasty farewells, I scampered off down to the dock and my waiting boatman. He'd just pulled in and seemed to be involved in some serious debate with a huddle of pelicans clustered around him. He looked at my sweaty shirt, earth-smudged face, and mosquito-ravaged arms, and gave a little beery smile.

"Enjoy your visit, then?"

20. Big Pine

"Take only memories; leave only footprints."

The air of the Florida Keys was spongy-moist. I was on Big Pine Island sitting in a patch of shade on the edge of an old limestone quarry pond. The water was still as oil, slick and black. They call it Blue Hole but there was little sign of blue. Leaves dangled listlessly from the normally effusive palms. A fat fish eased to the surface, released a flutter of air bubbles, and sank down slowly into the murkiness; smaller fish drifted lethargically among the reeds.

I sat waiting for Allig, the resident alligator.

And then he was there, drifting up from the depths like a worn branch ten feet from where I was sheltering from the heat. Sneaky. His ribbed hide seemed as ancient as the earth, a dusty dark gray. One eye was half closed in sleepy wariness and the tip of his snout protruded an inch above the surface. All the tales about alligators being mistaken for logs made sense—a more wooden creature is hard to imagine.

According to the wardens on Big Pine there are more than 300 alligators in ponds and sink holes in the National Key Deer Refuge plus a few specimens of American crocodile. Blue Hole itself claims a resident population of four with an average length of around 5 feet. "They're pretty docile," one of the rangers told me, "so long as they're left alone. One kid got herself into a spot of trouble though when she started throwing stones at Allig."

"What happened?" (nice juicy story here, I thought).

"Just what you'd expect. Allig-ate-her."

Rangers must have their little jokes too. Life is hard on the Big Pine refuges where residents, hunters, developers, and local politicians seem to be in constant conflict with the federal government on the status of these last acres of untouched Florida Keys. Part of the area has been set aside as a Great White Heron National Wildlife Refuge to provide safe breeding grounds for this graceful and dangerously-depleted species. The remainder is part of the National Key Deer Refuge in which around 500 tiny Key Deer, a subspecies of the Virginia White Tail deer, roam at random in a wilderness of slash pine, palms, sawgrass, and thornladen sweet acacia.

"Damn deer," one prickly Big Piner grumbled. "Every time they write somethin' about the damn deer they keep getting smaller. Now they've shrunk to 18 inches, smaller'n damn mutt."

Prior to the refuge, the diminutive size of the deer (top weight for a buck is 75 pounds with a shoulder height of 24-28 inches) was thought by most locals to be the result of poor diet, and hunters had few qualms about shooting them (although there wasn't very much meat on the little creatures). It took two people to make the difference. The first was gun-toting, cigar-chomping Jack Watson, who was a warden in the vast Everglades National Wildlife refuge in 1946 and sole agent in charge of the Big Pine area. His territory covered thousands of square miles and his job was to control poachers who preyed on everything from the easily captured doves sold as gourmet delicacies in Key West, to the ornery alligators whose hides brought premium prices in Eastern markets.

"It was a heck of a time," Jack explained. "I got shot at myself many times but I put most of them away. When I thought I might need to make a long shot I had myself a rifle. If it was going to be close work, I took my 12-gauge riot gun. Then there was my Thompson sub-machine gun and a 357 Magnum for a bit of a sidearm. They learned fast not to mess with me."

Jack was particularly concerned about the rapidly diminishing number of Key Deer and organized a count on Big Pine and No Name Keys.

"There was less than 50 still alive. You could go for weeks around here and never see one."

He and other enthusiasts pressed for action and in 1954 finally managed to pursuade legislators to establish the National Key Deer Refuge. Jack Watson, of course, was named man in charge but it still took five more years before the deer population began to increase significantly. Jack became known as "the man who saved the little deer" and the name stuck in part due to the influence of a second person, one of those "damn writers." Hope Ryden's delightful photographic book, "The Little Deer of the Florida Keys," brought national attention to their near-extinction and to the work of many groups trying to ensure their survival. Since then the deer have increased ten-fold and (to the relief of conservationists) show no sign of competing in size with their larger northern cousins. Poaching has been almost wiped out although every year more than 50 of the tiny creatures are killed by speeding cars on Route 1 and the road north to the tip of Big Pine.

"Allig" in the Blue Hole

"It's sad but you always get your racers on that road," Don Kosin, warden at the information center near Blue Hole, told me. "We don't want to keep people out. The refuges are meant for them; they love wandering around watching the deer and the alligators and those tiny racoons over on No Name Key. You may not see many deer till sundown, though. Try up by the subdivisions on the west side. They usually hang around the houses waiting for dinner. We asked the people not to feed them but what the heck can you do—it's their property. And it seems the deer have got an appetite now for gourmet meals."

After my brief sojourn at Blue Hole in the company of Allig, I took the road through the jungle-like vegetation towards No Name Key. I went as far east as I could and ended up on a coral promontory overlooking a turquoise bay dotted with tiny islands. Three crusty old pelicans waddled hopefully towards me and a heron stood stick-still in the shallows, pretending to be invisible. The promontory had once been a dock of sorts but nothing much remained except wooden stumps in the rock.

I swung the car around and returned along the broad straight road until a movement in the scrub made me pull over. Hardly had I stepped from the car than a score of small racoons lolloped out of the gloom and surrounded me, obviously awaiting tasty handouts. Don Kosin had told me about their antics and suggested I avoid feeding them. "They're friendly enough but they've got problems telling where food ends and fingers begin. And a racoon bite can be dangerous. You'll be in for a lousy set of rabies shots if you mess with them. Best to smile nicely and get out as fast as you can."

The racoons crowded in, circling my legs and looking ominous with bandit-like bands across their eyes and waving paws (beautifully detailed fingers with long claws). I moved back slowly, talking softly, but they somehow managed to keep the circle intact. It took a lively hop to leapfrog their snouts and scramble into the driver's seat. They stood forlornly in a cluster as I pulled away.

At the northern tip of Big Pine, where the road ends abruptly, I wandered off along a path through thorny acacia bushes to the edge of the island. Sharp ridges of gray-white coral made walking difficult and intricate webs of crab spiders (just like tiny crabs—spikes and all) kept getting tangled in my hair. Thick clumps of mangroves rose from the shallow salt water, and two white egrets picked and plucked among the reeds on the edge of a small inlet.

More than 250 species of birds have been recorded on Big Pine; I wanted to photograph the rare roseate spoonbill which a warden had spotted a few days previously in this quiet part of the island.

There were no sounds except the slappy ripples of sea and the dry clicking of lizards scampering across the coral; the mosquitoes and other biting nuisances were resting somewhere, waiting for a cooler dusk and dreaming of acres of exposed flesh. So I sat and slowly eased into reveries as the afternoon moved gently on, wafted by the breezes and a butterfly or two. I never did see a roseate spoonbill but it really didn't matter.

Later, as the heat eased, I drove a couple of miles south to explore the Pine Woods Trail, a carefully preserved wilderness of pine and palms on the edge of Watson Hammock, one of a handful of hardwood areas in the tropical Keys. More exhaustive research by local wardens and naturalists has produced a list of over 300 species of plant life along or near this third-of-a-mile trail: strange air plants, sixteen different types of orchids, butterwood, Jamaican dogwood, gumbo limbo, the notorious poisonwood (whose sap can cause a skin irritation worse than poison ivy), silver palm, and the painful sawgrass that can lacerate legs and arms with its sharp blades.

The trail curled past muddy sinkholes where water has dissolved the underlying layers of rock, leaving the surface to subside. Soil and seeds collect in the depressions and soon begin the familiar life-death-rot-life cycle which perpetuates growth in an otherwise difficult enviroment, and provides watering places for the animals of the forest. Smaller solution holes, usually less than a foot across, are leached out by surface water which slowly eats into the limestone, creating miniature breeding grounds for pine ferns and bracken. The vegetation changes constantly. A fall in elevation of less than two feet (high point on the island is nine feet, three inches) can attract wet soil grasses, butterwoods, and hardwoods; the higher, drier parts where topsoil tends to be shallower, are more conducive to the broad-rooted pines and hardy palms.

Special access can usually be arranged with the wardens into Watson Hammock, a deep soil area ideal for hardwoods and once home of the Calusa Indians. They built a permanent settlement here, Cuchiyaga, and lived off abundant local fish, berries, and venison. After the arrival of Spanish settlers they became aggressive and were eventually wiped out in the mid 1800s.

I met a young California couple on my stroll along the Pine Woods Trail who had spent the morning snorkeling on the south side of Big Pine. A coral reef known as Looe Key, named after a 44 cannon British frigate, HMS Looe, wrecked here in 1744, provides some of the best diving outside the famed John Pennekamp Coral Reef at the northern end of the Keys.

One of the tiny
Key Deer
on Big Pine

"Fantastic!" Eric told me as his all-California-girl gazed at him adoringly. "There are cliffs, forty—fifty feet vertical, covered in coral—all different colors. And some salt coral too. Feels like sponge. And the fish! Man! I've never seen so many parrot fish. And grouper—I counted eighteen plus a whole cliff-side of tiny octopuses. It's another world down there—yeah, I know, that's what you hear them all say but you've got to go down to feel it—to believe it. Just fantastic!"

I decided to leave snorkeling until my visit to the Dry Tortugas, way out in the Gulf beyond Key West. The sun was reddening and it was deer-spotting time, so I drove back up Big Pine and into a half finished subdivision facing out across the lagoon. All the houses were built on ten foot high stilts, apparently a local regulation following the devastation of a hurricane in 1964. At first I was disappointed. There was little sign of life beyond the occasional yapping dog and an elderly couple highballing on their terrace, watching the dropping sun.

Then I spotted five deer, two adults and three youngsters trotting behind like pet pups. They were in the shade by the side of a large white-walled villa munching on scraps left by the residents. They seemed very tame and as I moved closer to photograph them, they came towards me, presumably for more tasty tidbits. But I'd taken Don's advice and brought no food. The buck, hardly more than waist high, yet perfectly mature, with a magnificent set of antlers, gave me a disgusted look and signalled his family to move on and ignore this mean intruder. I followed them, clicking away as the light went out of the sun. They stayed a safe distance and showed no interest in my photographic antics—all except for one of the young ones who seemed more than happy to show off for the camera. Father shook his antlers, gave a little snort, and the errant creature rejoined the family group as they eased through the high grass into the palmetto. The young one gave me one last look, wagged his white tail, and vanished.

It will not be easy for refuge staff to protect these creatures from the ravages of developers who have by no means given up their fight to turn Big Pine into a typical Florida key filled with shining subdivisions, shopping malls, and parking lots. One can only hope that visitors will return home impressed by what has been accomplished and will press for tighter legislation and more generous funding for the refuges.

Meanwhile they should "take only memories; leave only footprints," and enjoy one of the last unspoiled keys in Florida.

An elderly pelican (and bowlegged too!)

21. The Dry Tortugas

Blue Paradise

From 500 feet up you float down like a spiral-riding seagull, down out of the blue into more blues—turquoise, azure, aquamarine, sky, streaks of royal and near-purple—to the surf-tatty edges of reefs. Infinity in both directions. Curlicues of blue-white sand sixty feet down under a ripple-topped ocean, and hints, tantalizing hints, of deeper and deeper worlds littered with rainbowed parrot fish, tarpon, barracuda, slow-rolling manta rays, sharks, and even the occasional cluster of whales.

In 1513, if Ponce de Leon had flown in as we did, he might have dreamed up a better name than "Dry Tortugas." Dry referred to a lack of fresh water; Tortugas tells us he found a lot of turtles. His men feasted on turtle steaks and moved on—ever onwards—in search of the elusive fountain of youth. The Dry Tortugas continued their slumber, pleasing only to the Gods.

Key West, the jewel-like "Conch Republic," is well out of sight and mind. Goodbye to the oh-so earnest Hemingway-hunters at Sloppy Joe's, Captain Tony's, and various other imitations of his favorite bars adorned with slow-churning fans, bamboo slats, yellowed clippings of "Pappy" legends, and miscellaneous props of a dubious heritage. Goodbye to the pretty hangouts filled with gays in tight white jeans and touch-me T-shirts (a summertime Christopher Street); the porno-pits trying to look enticingly decadent but managing merely decadent; the ragged palms shading ragged filigree eaves. Goodbye to the sponge shops; shrimp boats; the precious refinement of the Pier House hotel ("oh darling—this is just the way I thought it would be"); the be-bop boozed-out slum shanties; the ominously pristine-clean cemeteries so bright they burn your eyeballs; the dishes of golden conch fritters (remarkably tasteless meat for all the local hype); the sunset rituals on the dock with magicians, jugglers, singers, raconteurs and pretty hook-for-hash dropouts mellowed on sticky, sleepy heat and warm rum.

Goodbye to all that for a few blue hours out on the islands sixty-odd miles west. It's a $75 day and worth every cent.

There are eight of them, plus a thousand coral stumps and ledges. The tiny plane lands in a haze of spray at Garden Key; a flurry of startled sooty terns on

HAPPY HOUR!! 4-7

PINA COLADA

Irrepressible Key West

Bush Key fly up, wheel erratically, and flop back into the sandy scrub. A few shrimp boats, nets raised and sagging like droopy angel's wings, wait for night and scoops of "pink gold" to fill the coffers.

The pilot has told his pirate tales. They were all here at one time or another during the free-for-all centuries when the Spanish galleons looted the Americas and returned home via the Florida Straits and the easy-sailing Gulf Stream—Edward "Blackbeard" Teach, Jose Gaspar, Captain William Kidd, Sir Henry Morgan, Bartholomew Sharp, "Black Caesar," and a score of less-known privateers roaming the Caribbean in search of booty, and using the Tortugas as a convenient and secluded base.

Treasure, of course, is said to be buried here—millions in bars of silver and gold, and bulging leather bags filled with jewels, pearls, semi-precious stones, and pieces of eight. If the legends ever lag, someone inevitably revives them with a fresh "discovery" of gold coins. And even though the pirates are long-gone, mercilessly hounded down by Commodore David Porter after the War of 1812, tales of more modern-day scoundrels—the salvage-wreckers, gun-and-rum runners, drug-smugglers, alien-shippers and criminals on the loose—keep the mystery and magic of the Dry Tortugas alive and well in this balmy paradise.

Except for a 150 foot high lighthouse on Loggerhead Key, the century-old bastion of Fort Jefferson on Garden Key is the only structure of any significance on the islands. This gray-pink monolith, a brooding hexagon of stern architectural refinement, was one of the largest forts on the American continent. Construction costs in the late 1800s ran over three and a half million dollars and even after 30 years the place was still unfinished. Two hundred and forty three elephantine cannons, each more than 20 feet long, thrust their black snouts out from the battlements, but not once were they fired in anger.

The place was never used as a fort, although President James Polk was convinced of the need to protect the new nation's soft underbelly when he authorized construction of this "Gibraltar of America" in 1846. Hundreds of laborers, mostly black slaves, suffered the outrageous sun, hurricanes, scurvy, dysentery, and the savagery of the local mosquitoes, to build the 60 foot high edifice with a total rampart length of almost a mile, a fifteen foot deep moat (later filled with sharks and barracuda), a huge outer sea wall, and even the medieval accoutrements of heavy baronial gates and drawbridge.

An observer at the time noticed that "the building conditions at Fort Jefferson were a hundred-fold worse than must have existed during the erection of

Egypt's pyramids." More than 40 million bricks were used in construction and the ornate detailing of the officers' quarters within the 16 acre compound indicates an exceptional quality of craftsmanship. But the invention of powerful rifled cannons which could pierce even the thickest walls made the place obsolete. It was used instead as a Civil War prison for around 1,000 inmates.

The most notorious occupant was Dr. Samuel A. Mudd who was sentenced to life imprisonment for setting John Wilkes Booth's broken leg after the assassination of Lincoln. Mudd arrived here in 1865, and after one abortive escape attempt, was relegated to a "brutal and degrading" dungeon and kept in leg irons for almost two years until a rampant yellow fever epidemic hit the fort. When the garrison surgeon, Major Joseph S. Smith, was stricken with the disease, Mudd was asked to take his place and worked 20 hour days, "as in some horrible nightmare," trying to comfort and save the other inmates and officers. Scores died before Mudd finally eradicated the pestilence. His work and perseverence were praised by all survivors who petitioned the government for a pardon, but he had to wait a further three years, until 1869, before President Andrew Johnson issued the pardon and had him returned home.

After his release the fort was abandoned except for a small Coast Guard station. The battleship "Maine" paused for refueling here in 1898 before resuming her ill-fated journey to Havana Harbor where she was sunk by a series of mysterious explosions. The fort gradually slipped into neglect and disrepair, battered by hurricanes, a refuge for sailors in sudden summer storms, an ideal rendezvous for modern day pirates and drug-smugglers.

Today the place is run by the National Park Service and retains its air of gloomy mystery. Wind-ripped roofs, tangled beams, and decades of elaborate graffiti seem a sad end for such a monumental piece of engineering. They say over 300 slaves died building this place and as you walk the high battlements among the black cannons, peering out at that incredible blue ocean and watching for sharks in the moat sixty feet below, you can hear the wind screaming through the wall cracks and the narrow cell windows—a haunting, mournful sound that sends shivers down to your toes.

Fortunately there are other distractions here, most notably the vast colonies of terns on Bush Key and other smaller shoals. During the April to September nesting season millions of excitable sooty and noddy terns nurse their eggs and offspring while enormous frigate birds, with wingspans of up to seven feet, soar on the thermals, occasionally diving earthward to snatch an

Dry Tortugas

eggy snack. Audubon made a visit here in 1833 from his Key West base and spent days strolling and sketching the teeming colonies.

Often included in the cost of boat and plane excursions is an hour or two of snorkeling among the brilliantly-colored coral reefs. There's even an under-water "trail" marked out for novices, where you can tickle the bellies of the parrot fish and play Cousteau in the limpid pools before flopping on the beach and whiling away the rest of the afternoon.

And then it's back home again for the sunset celebrations down by the Key West dock. We fly low over the purpling waters; the pilot points at a couple of sunken wrecks clearly visible among the reefs. A manta ray moves like a slow shadow through the shallows, and shrimp boats bob in a gently rolling ocean. In the far distance, I can see the chain of keys and scores of deep green jigsaw shapes edged in white.

More mysterious islands; more places to explore...

Island Access and Accommodation

The following information was checked for accuracy in 1984, but prices, times and other details often change annually so it's best to call in advance.
During the peak summer season ferry reservations are usually necessary if you plan on taking a car, and hotel reservations are always recommended.

1. ST. PIERRE-MIQUELON

Access By Air:
From Halifax, Nova Scotia, daily flight during summer season; Monday, Wednesday, and Friday at other times. Call (902) 861-4916 for details and reservations.
From Sydney, Nova Scotia, daily flight (except Sundays) during summer season with Air St. Pierre; Tuesdays and Saturdays only at other times. Call (902) 562-3140. $100 round trip.

Access By Boat:
From Halifax, Nova Scotia, once a week with Newfoundland Container Lines (902) 422-7451. $80 round trip.
From Fortune, Newfoundland, daily return trips with Lake Lloyd Trips, (709) 832-1955. $35 round trip.
For latest information call the Goora Travel Service in North Sydney at (902) 794-4800.

Accommodation
Abundant hotels, pensions and restaurants in all price ranges. Complete details from St. Pierre-Miquelon Tourist Office, Place du General de Gaulle, St. Pierre; The Goora Travel Service, North Sydney, Nova Scotia, (902) 794-4800, or The French Government Tourist Office, 610 Fifth Avenue, New York, NY 10020, (212) 757-1125.

Entry Requirements
U.S. Citizens do not require passports. Driving licence or other I.D. is adequate.

2. THE MAGDALEN ISLANDS

Access By Air:

Daily flights are available from Montreal and Quebec by Quebecair, (514) 636-3890, and Eastern Provincial Airways, (514) 631-9431, but the most popular link is by daily 5 hour ferry at 2 p.m. from Souris on Prince Edward Island (80 auto capacity/300 passengers). No reservations for outgoing trip and delays may be at least a day in summer. Return reservations are suggested during summer, (418) 986-2214. Adults $14 each way; children 5-12 $7; children under 5 free. Auto $27 each way. Additional information from C.T.M.A. Ferry, PO Box 245, Cap-Aux-Meules, Magdalen Islands, GOB 1 BO.

Access By Boat:

A regular two day freighter trip from Montreal is also available. There's only room for 15 passengers so reservations are required 2 months in advance by Voyages Frontenac, (514) 871-1686, and the all inclusive cost per person is $150 plus $75 for an auto.

Accommodation

The dozen or so hotels and motels are found mainly in Havre-aux-Maisons and Cap-aux-Meules. Among the best in Cap-aux-Meules are Auberge de laJetée ($20-35 for two); Chateau Madelinot ($20-30 for two) and the Motel Bellevue ($30 for two). Chalets, tourist homes and camping sites are also available at modest rates. A complete list can be obtained from the Commission Touristique, (418) 986-4251, or call toll-free in Quebec, 1-800-361-5405. Reservations are advisable.

Entry Requirements

The Canadian government requests you bring identification, driving license and insurance policy (or Canada Insurance card issued by your company). Pets may require special shots before entry.

---

3. GRAND MANAN

Access

Five summer ferry trips daily from Black's Harbor in Canada starting at 8 a.m. (3 trips on Sundays). Be prepared for delays. Trips before July 1 and after September 1 are less frequent. Autos $7; passengers $2, children $1. Snack bar on ferry. Information (506) 662-3306 or (506) 466-1139.

Accommodation

The four major hotels are all close to the ferry landing at North Head: The Marathon Inn (506-662-8144) from $35 single and $50 double including breakfast and dinner; The Compass Rose (506-662-8570), $14 single, $23 double including breakfast; The

Shorecrest Lodge (506-662-3216), $16 single, $19 double, (breakfast $2 and family-style dinner $8); Surfside Motel (506-662-8156) from $22 single and $28 double. Some furnished cottages are also available starting at $100 per week.

Services
Bike hire, whale-watching trips, (506) 662-8144, and fishing boat trips to the outer islands, (506) 662-8296. There are also plans for scuba diving parties to submerged wrecks.

Entry Requirements
Same as The Magdalen Islands.

---

4. DEER ISLAND

Access
Eastport Ferry only runs from late June—September 20 (car and driver $5; passengers $1). Campobello Ferry, a wonderful contraption of fishing boat and raft, runs from late June—Labor Day (car and driver $6, passengers 75¢.

The ferry from Lambertville, Deer Island, to Letete is free.

Accommodation
Hartford's Guest Home, (506) 747-2284, from $15 single and $20 double. 45th Parallel Motel, (506) 747-2231, call for details. Camping facilities $5 per day.

Entry Requirements
Same as the Magdalen Islands.

---

5. THE CRANBERRIES

Access
Regular *Sea Queen* trips June 21 - September 4 from Northeast Harbor: 10 a.m., noon, 3 p.m., 5:30 p.m., 8:30 p.m. (also special daily historical, whale and seabird, and evening dinner cruises in summer). Off season ferry: 11 a.m., 2:30 p.m., 4:30 p.m. $2.50 round trip; $1.50 children. Call Beal and Bunker Inc., (207) 244-3575, for further details.

Accommodation
Very scarce. Assume none unless reservations made well in advance. Contact Beal and Bunker for current details.

Other Facilities
Isleford Dock Restaurant on Little Cranberry; snacks and bike hire on Great Cranberry. No alcohol.

---

6. SWAN'S ISLAND

Access
Six daily round trips on weekends during summer from Bass Harbor from 7 a.m. - 5 p.m. (4 trips on Sunday). Reduced service off season (usually 4 round trips a day). $2.50 adult round trip; $1.50 children. $10.50 auto round trip with driver. Auto reservations recommended during summer (207) 526-4273 ($2.50 extra).

Accommodation
Occasional rooms and cottages by reservation. Call (207) 526-4404 for general information. No public camp grounds.

Other Facilities
2 or 3 small snack bars and take outs during summer season. "Sea Breeze" open all year. No alcohol.

7. VINALHAVEN

Access
2 round trips daily from Rockland during summer on weekdays (8:40 a.m. and 1:10 p.m.); Sundays 8:45 a.m. Off season round trip 9 a.m. $3.50 adult round trip. $2 children. $15.25 auto round trip with driver. Auto reservations recommended during summer, (207) 594-5543 ($2.50 extra).

Accommodation
The Tidewater Motel, Main Street, (207) 863-4618. Summer rates: single $25, double $37. Reservations recommended. Kitchen units also.

Other accommodations and cottage rentals are variable. Call (207) 863-4676 for information or write: Vinalhaven Development Association, Vinalhaven, ME 04863

Other Facilities
3 snack bar/restaurants in village; bike and moped rentals available.

NOTE:
Regular Vinalhaven event is the Lobster and Clam Bake every Wednesday and Sunday, noon—4 p.m. during summer, $10 per person and worth it. No alcohol.

8. MONHEGAN

Access
From Port Clyde: Leaves 10 a.m. and 2:30 p.m., daily June 22 to September 23; 10 a.m. daily except Sunday in spring and fall, and Monday, Wednesday and Friday at 10 a.m. in winter. Round trip fare: Adults $14; Children under 12, $7. Call (207) 372-8848 for

details and reservations.

No cars.

From Boothbay Harbor: Leaves 9:15 a.m. daily, June 10 to September 25. Round trip fare: Adults $18; children under 10, $14. Also island cruises on arrival. Call (207) 633-2284 for details and reservations.

From New Harbor: Leaves weekends only at 9:30 a.m., from July 4—Labor Day. Round trip fare: Adults $9; children under 12, $6. Call (207) 799-1091 for details and reservations.

Accommodation

The Island Inn, (207) 596-0371; Monhegan House, (207) 594-7983; Trailing Yew, (207) 596-0440.

No camping allowed. Other guest houses and private accommodation also available year round.

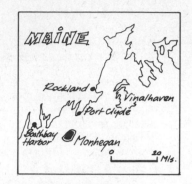

9. CLIFF ISLAND

Access

Monday through Friday at 5:20 a.m. 10 a.m., 2:30 p.m. and 5:30 p.m.; Saturday 7 a.m., 10 a.m., and 2 p.m.; Sunday 10 a.m. and 2 p.m. from Custom House Wharf in Portland, Maine. Round Trip for adults $5; children under 9, $2.75. Additional details from Casco Bay Lines at (207) 774-7871.

Accommodation

None

10. ISLES OF SHOALS

Access

Viking Queen from Portstmouth daily during summer season (May—October) at 11 a.m. and 2 p.m. Adults $10; children under 12, $8, including guided tour. Crossing time (narrated cruise) 2½ hours. Also other "early bird" and "dinner cruises" normally offered during summer. Call (603) 431-5500 for latest details.

Accommodation

Only for organized research groups or religious conferences.

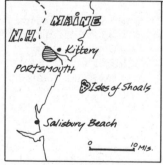

11. CUTTYHUNK

Access

From New Bedford: summer schedule, (June 16—September 15), Monday—Friday 10 a.m., returning by 4:30 p.m. Weekends 9 a.m.. Crossing time 1½ hours. Adults $10 round trip; children under 12 half fare. Winter schedule: Tuesday and Friday only, 10 a.m. returning by 3:30 p.m. Call Cuttyhunk Boat Lines at (617) 992-1432 for details.

Accommodation

Allen House. Call (617)996-9292 for details and reservations.

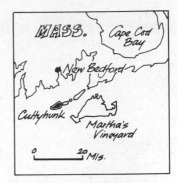

12. PRUDENCE

Access

The ferry leaves from Bristol 5 times most days during the summer starting at 7 a.m. (6 a.m. on Mondays; 8 a.m. at weekends); less frequently off season. Adults $2.35 one way; children under 12, 90¢,for a 40 minute crossing with dockings at Hog Island, Homestead and Sandy Point. No cars. Bring bikes, hire them on the island, or just walk. Call (401) 245-7411 for latest details.

Accommodation

With the exception of a few weekly rental cabins, usually booked well in advance by regulars, Prudence Inn is the island's only accommodation and restaurant (open May 15 - November 30). Single with private bath and breakfast $35; double $70. Special rates for children and "Weekender" packages available. No credit cards, and no alcohol served although guests may bring their own and automatically become members of the Prudence Point Island Club! Maps, bikes and inexpensive island transportatioin are also available. Call (401) 683-9893 or 884-4188 for reservations.

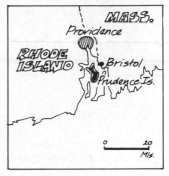

13. SMITH ISLAND

Access

Captain Alan Tyler's cruise boat leaves daily from Somers Cove Marina in Crisfield: 12:30 a.m.—5:15 p.m.; $12 return; docking at Rhodes Point for optional lunch, and bus ride to Ewell: Memorial Day through September. Call (301) 425-2771 for reservations. Also the mailboat sails from the town wharf ($5 return; docking at Ewell, optional lunch); it gets you there faster and gives you more time for exploration. Captain Tyler believes people come to enjoy the ocean journey just as much as the island itself and so he takes a good hour each way.

Accommodation

Frances Kitching offers bed, breakfast and dinner in her delightful guest house for around $35 per person. Call (301) 425-3321 for details and reservations.

Other accommodation is occasionally available at Rhodes Point.

14. TANGIER ISLAND

Access

From Crisfield, Maryland: Daily 12:30—5:15 p.m. Memorial Day—October 31. $12 adults; $6 children under 12. call (301) 968-2338 or (804) 891-2240 for details.

From Reedville, Virginia:
Daily 10:00 a.m. - 4:15 p.m. May 1 - October 15.
$16 adults; $8 children 4 - 12; free for children under 4; call (804) 333-4656 for details.

At other times there is a daily mail boat service (except Sundays October—May) from Crisfield at 12:30 p.m. returning the following morning at 8:00 a.m.

A ferry route from Hancock, Virginia on the southern Delmarva peninsula is still in the experimental stage and its future undecided.

Accommodation

Simple overnight accommodation can be reserved April 1—October 31 at Chesapeake House at $30 per person including a family style dinner (similar to the huge lunch), and an enormous family style breakfast. Call (804) 891-2331.

15. OCRACOKE

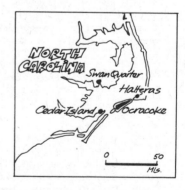

Access

From Cape Hatteras: Free car and passenger ferry across Hatteras Inlet every 40 minutes from 5 a.m.—11 p.m., April 15—October 31; during the winter season every hour on the hour from 5 a.m.—5 p.m. and at 7, 9 and 11 p.m.

From Swan Quarter, N.C.: Twice a day all year at 9:30 a.m. and 4 p.m. Cars up to 20', $10. Passengers $1. Call (919) 926-1111 for reservations (recommended). Crossing time 2½ hours.

From Cedar Island, N.C.: Summer ferry five times a day at 7 a.m., 9:20 a.m., 11:40 a.m., 2 p.m. and 4:20 p.m.; less frequent at other times. Cars up to 20', $10. Passengers $1. Call (919) 225-3551 for reservations (recommended). Crossing time 2½ hours.

Accommodation

Ample motel accommodation in Ocracoke village. Call (919) 928-4531 for details. Camping also available.

16. CAPE LOOKOUT

Access

From Harkers Island: daily 9 a.m. and 1 p.m. in summer; less regular off-season. Call (919) 728-3575. Adults $8 round trip; children 5—10, $4 (under 4, $1). Beach transportation also available.

From Atlantic: Daily 7 a.m., 11 a.m., and 3 p.m. in season. Call (919) 225-4261 for details, prices and reservations. Special tours of Portsmouth Village also.

From Davis: Flexible schedule. Call (919) 729-2791.

Accommodation

Primitive camping facilities only. Call National Park Service in Beaufort, N.C., (919) 728-2121 or (919) 728-2250. Additional details from Carteret County Chamber of Commerce, (919) 726-6831.

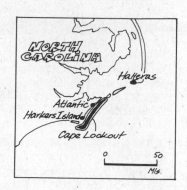

17. DAUFUSKIE

Access

Arrangements keep changing but ferries normally leave from Harbor Town or Palmetto Bay Marina on Hilton Head Island daily except Sunday. Call either (803) 785-3311 or (803) 842-4155 for latest details and prices. Some trips include an organized tour and/or lunch.

Accommodation

None available.

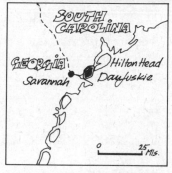

18. SAPELO

Access

Special State-run ferry from Meridian. Cost $2 round trip; times and tours are variable. Call The Georgia Department of Natural Resources at (912) 264-7330 for latest details.

Accommodation

None, unless special research-trip arrangements are made in advance with the appropriate State or University departments.

LIGNUMVITAE

Access
Private ferry service available. (Go with a group if possible otherwise the normal $5 fee can increase dramatically!) A public ferry may be provided in the near future.

Accommodation
No accommodation available on the island but ample choice along Route 1.

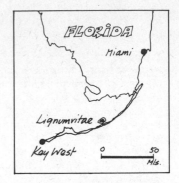

BIG PINE

Access
Directly off Route 1 on Big Pine Key. No ferry required.

Accommodations
Abundant motels along Route 1.

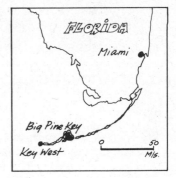

21. DRY TORTUGAS

Access
Various companies offer day trips by seaplane or boat and advance reservations are usually unnecessary. Call the Key West Tourist Information Office at (305) 294-2587 or (305) 566-0700 for latest details. Plane trips normally around $75 round trip.

Accommodation
No hotels but camping is usually permitted.
Call the Tourist Office (above) for details.

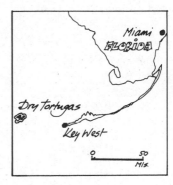